ELVIS IS TITANIC

ELVIS IS TITANIC

Classroom Tales from
the Other Iraq

IAN KLAUS

Alfred A. Knopf
New York
2007

This Is a Borzoi Book
Published by Alfred A. Knopf

Knopf, Borzoi Books, and the colophon are registered
trademarks of Random House, Inc.

Grateful acknowledgment is made to Alfred A. Knopf
for permission to reprint "The Negro Speaks
of Rivers" from *The Collected Poems of Langston
Hughes,* edited by Arnold Rampersad with David
Roessel, copyright © 1994 by The Estate of Langston
Hughes. Reprinted by permission of Alfred A. Knopf,
a division of Random House, Inc.

Library of Congress Cataloging-in-Publication Data
Klaus, Ian, [date]
Elvis is Titanic : classroom tales from the other
Iraq / by Ian Klaus.—1st ed.
p. cm.
ISBN 978-0-307-26456-5
1. Education, Higher—Iraq—Kurdistan. 2. Teachers,
Foreign—Iraq—Kurdistan. 3. College teachers—United States.
4. Kurdistan (Iraq)—Politics and government—21st century.
5. Iraq War, 2003– I. Title.
LA1469.K87K58 2007
370.956.7'2—dc22   2007006807

Manufactured in the United States of America
First Edition

To my mother and Chelsea, for understanding

Of course we know who Elvis is. Elvis is *Titanic*.

CONTENTS

Introduction   3

ELVIS IS TITANIC

Introduction

ARMIES have never gone abroad alone. They have been accompanied by political officers, reporters, adventurers, opportunists, and intellectuals. Always in tow have been thinkers who travel, and travelers who write, bold young individuals out to make their names and old ones who've long since lost their sense of home. Some writers, historians, and philologists who followed armies have come to be called imperialists or Orientalists. By whatever name, I, too, was treading in the footsteps of soldiers, some of whom I had called roommates and friends. They, like me, had once been Rhodes scholars and had followed America's campaign to Afghanistan and Iraq.

I came to Iraq on the eve of the first election in January 2005, not intending to write but hoping to teach. After what some would call liberation and during what most would call occupation, I began to teach American history and English at one of the country's largest universities. Was it foolish or reckless for an American to be in Iraq at this moment leading discussions on American history? Perhaps. Maybe it was imperialist in a small way. But if I hadn't been there, who would have answered the young man who asked, "Why does America only go where there is oil?" Who would have taught English to Mohammed, a young Islamist who held down two jobs and had resolved to acquire the language long before I arrived?

Would someone else have written about Trefa, a Kirkuki

woman in her early twenties who had lost her older brother to
Saddam's terror, who, for religious reasons, would not shake
hands with men but had no more cherished dream than to
study in America? Or about Mahir: this son of an imam who
denounced music had nonetheless become one of Iraqi Kurdistan's beloved pop stars.

It was in this setting, among the Kurds and at Salahaddin
University in Arbil, that I began to write. Kurdistan was, in fact,
the great counterfactual: the region that the Iraqi National
Congress and other opposition groups in exile hoped to use as a
model, as something of a foundation for the rest of the country.
It still endured shootings and bombings, but its fledgling democratic and economic institutions as well as its process of political
reconciliation were operating in relatively stable conditions. Its
people, for the most part, admired America. In some ways, this
was the way it was supposed to be.

It is there, and amid the larger conversations about democracy and theocracy, about ancient faiths, and about America and
the world, that this book is set. Indeed, in almost every classroom I entered, America was the first topic raised—and not
because I brought it up.

These tales are not intended as either analysis or objective
reportage. They are merely stories of love lost and souls on hold,
of people born anew and others newly disenchanted. They are
situated in a complicated time and place, but also suffused with
emotions that can be felt and understood anywhere.

It may be that those I came to know in Iraqi Kurdistan can
only be partially illuminated, silhouettes in the swirling Iraqi
dust, shrouded like so many specters in the evening shadow of
Kurdish mountains. Even in the context of the most rational and
respectful conversation, even in friendship, there are limits to
mutual comprehension. But it is precisely because we speak of
individual lives—of aspirations and dreams, dashed hopes and

unexpected resurrections—that we must try. "What the history of ordinary life delivers is the shock of recognition—my kind is human kind," wrote the American historian Joyce Appleby.[1] Hence here are the stories and thoughts of my students, mostly in their own words, who became my friends and who, like all good friends, also became my teachers.

1. Beyond War

"INCOMING text message."

Class had let out and I was making my way across the city from one of the university's campuses to another when I started to receive text messages from students I had dismissed not fifteen minutes before. It was a short walk, and though some of my friends preferred that I not take it alone, I picked my way through the more heavily guarded sections of Arbil, capital of the Kurdistan region of Iraq. Students on cell phones passed, kicking up dust on newly paved asphalt; security guards settled into their chairs in front of blast walls, sharing observations about the city's construction cranes. Text messages kept coming.

"Bounty? NO! Kit Kat? NEVER! Mars? . . . How about sugar?? Still can't find anything as sweet as you!"

Almost a year after first arriving in Iraq to teach American history and English, I had returned to the same university in Kurdistan to present a couple of lessons on American education and language. Moving across the city that day, trying to gather my bearings, I found myself as acutely aware of the fortifications and arms as I had been twelve months before: Why is that building so heavily guarded? Who is in that winding convoy? Is it wise to be staying in a hotel made of glass? The anxious imagination as perpetual motion machine—what catches my eye is commonplace to the locals. The bus drivers picking up familiar passengers, the cabbies gossiping at black-market gas stations, the storekeepers in the bazaar were not likely to be talking about checkpoints and armored vehicles. The students on cell phones, too, had concerns of their own beyond the Kalashnikovs that over the decades had become so ubiquitous they were almost invisible. Other forces, beyond those of bristling militarism, were busy at work.

My phone kept vibrating with new messages.

"Triangles have 3 ends. Lines have 2 ends. Life has one end. But our friendship has no ends."

Flirtatious, solicitous, and curious, all of the incoming messages testified to a hope of engagement, as much with the wider world as with me, its apparent proxy. After another class later that same day, I spent an hour chatting with a dozen or so students keen to work on their conversation skills. Most who hung around peppered me with questions about home, my favorite movies, and my views of the relative merits of Michael Jackson and Shakira. One young man, however, interjected to talk about himself and his goals. Slightly shorter than the rest, he was notably tanned, considering the winter season, and a bit pockmarked. He was in his final year at the university but wanted to continue to improve his English. With a heavily bearded and expressionless classmate looming over him, the young man described his plans: upon graduation, he would move to Mosul to work with U.S. forces. Translators, like all Iraqis working with Western media outlets, had been hunted, targeted, and killed by the dozens. Though aware of the dangers, he still considered this the best, indeed the only, route available to further develop his language skills. My phone continued to vibrate in my suit pocket.

Incoming text message: "If the sun forget the earth . . . If fats forget food . . . If heart forget beating . . . If valentine forget love . . . If Bush forget Bin Laden . . . but, I never forget you."

To counter terror. To develop democracy. To serve capitalism. To spread freedom. The intentions of the American invasion of

Iraq were articulated in relation to no few American ideals. But for these students, a single concern was paramount: opportunity. Opportunity to learn, to pursue contacts, or a career not determined by the state; and, finally, opportunity to be part of an independent Kurdistan. Their parents had suffered violently and bitterly under Saddam Hussein. And they had watched as the dictator was deposed with overwhelming power and violence. Now, this generation's engagement with power was something different: amid violence and corruption, hope was diffused through cell phones and satellite dishes, meted out by markets and new parliaments.

"I want to practice my English and I can't do it anywhere else," the young man insisted. "I will take my chances with the terrorists."

2. How and Why: Feet on the Ground, Head in the Sky

When you reach the threshold of the great gateway
There's a bustle of retainers, and folks gather round,
They guide you through to the hall,
Then all is hospitality and welcome to the guest;
The corps of retainers, bandoliers slung on shoulders,
Heads and hats swollen with bright silken turbans,
Hands upon daggers, awaiting their orders,
Be they to chop off a head or bring in dinner . . .

—Kurdish poet Mirza Abdullah Goran, translated
by C. J. Edmonds, political officer of Her Majesty's
Foreign Service, 1919–1925

TWELVE months before, in February 2005, the head of the history department at Salahaddin University had given me a five-minute introduction and then left me alone with a translator in front of fifty rather bewildered students.

"Mamosta [teacher] Ian, what are you doing here?" a male student in the back of the class quickly asked before I could speak.

Young men in tight-fitting bell-bottoms or jeans streaked unevenly with bleach filled half the seats. Some shirts shimmered; on others the collar points drooped down halfway to the wearer's shoulders. Footwear ranged from cowboy boots to knockoff Italian square-toed loafers, the whole scene a remarkable fashion hybrid: Middle Eastern, American Western, Roman boulevardier. Women, who would wear fabulous outfits of color and glitter some months later for graduation, were now heavily made up and bundled in coats against the winter's cold. A gang of black-clad young men, some with full beards, quietly looked on from the back of the classroom. (Some of these more religious students would prove to be good students and even better people; others would not.) A few stragglers came in, pronouncing their apologies, their stories belied by small smiles of mischief. Cell phones vibrated on desks as ringtones of the latest Syrian songs filtered through pockets and handbags.

A barrage of various forms of the same question soon followed. A young man asked, "We mean, what are you doing in Kurdistan, not just at the university?"

The question was not unreasonable. After all, in a city and a country that had seen decades of war, where regional stability was precarious and the history of oppression and a sense of limited options weighed on every student, a classroom was not a place to expect strangers. It was, to be sure, a classroom in Kurdistan—a place where secularism had a strong toehold and virtual national autonomy had been established for nearly a decade and a half, but it was also in Iraq, where sectarian violence was fast becoming the daily norm.

"What do you think of Kurdistan? And how do you make out of the university?" one student ventured shyly in broken English. He added, "You are very welcome to Kurdistan. And thank you. And I want to talk about America too." The United States had "liberated" them, to use a word floated freely by the Kurds in reference to the toppling of Saddam. American movies and consumer products were rapidly appearing in the bazaar. But despite the dramatic changes resulting from American foreign policy and economic might, I was the first American that most of these young men and women had ever met.

Behind the lectern, a faded map of Iraq, with the region of Kurdistan outlined, hung near the eraser board. Next to it, another map showed North Africa and the greater Mediterranean, including southern Europe, with the Middle East highlighted in bright green. These were the visual aids for what would be the first class in American history for the young Kurds, whose capacity to look West was restrained because they were in Iraq.

Four days before the January 30, 2005, elections, I had crossed into Iraq. Four hours north of the border is Diyarbakir, the southeastern Turkish city into which one flies when entering Iraq from the north. It has long been a stronghold of Kurdish nationalism and militancy in Turkey—this was true Anatolia, the East, a world away from the thriving cosmopolitan metropolis on the Bosporus. The plains stretching out around Diyarbakir soon give way to dusty and crumbling mountains as one heads south to the border.

This is a historic cradle of humanity, and the local people lay active claim to its heritage. Mount Ararat, the supposed resting spot of Noah's ark, lies to the northeast, and to the southwest is Harran, the village in which Abraham first heard the voice of God. Taxi drivers, hoteliers, and soldiers alike tell tales linking them to millennia past as well as to stories common to the Koran, the Torah, and the Bible. A legend of Abraham's birth is juxtaposed with a spotting of the ark by Russian pilots during the First World War. In places one can make out the train track that in better times carried people into Syria; now it is obscured amid the rocks and weedy growth of the border no-man's-land. As one continues toward the border, the decaying past figures less prominently than the present checkpoints, and the minefields are more relevant to the future than stories. Like the dust, the roadside rubbish, and abandoned, broken-down vehicles, tokens of politics are ubiquitous; the overwhelming sense of nowhere is countered by reminders of geopolitics past and present. Every couple of hundred yards, there is evidence of stifled declarations of power and sovereignty, empty guard towers rising up from barren land.

In Silopi, a few miles before one officially crosses over into Iraq, an indiscriminate row of dirty shops stands apart from the road, fronted by a parking lot—an arrangement reminiscent of American strip malls. In the space where a sidewalk might have existed, a car, bombed out and half missing, is mounted on blocks. In the bustling chaos, one could easily miss the wreck; but if one happens to look out one's left-side window, the image is not easily forgotten. The rear tires are raised an extra two feet to give a full view of the ruined undercarriage. The car is a symbol, a menacing signpost to the wayward pilgrim. The bombing may well have been the work of a Kurdish separatist group, but whoever the agent, the act was meant to encourage some and deter others. It is, in fact, an advertisement of violence on the route into Iraq initially favored by American military planners, before the war started in March 2003. With Jordan and Syria unwilling to grant passage to American troops, and the Saudi government increasingly riven by violent internal struggle over, in part, relations with America, only three potentially feasible routes could be imagined for an American invasion. The Kuwait-Iraq border was a likely one. Iraq's own short seacoast provided only limited access. The third way was through Turkey. Turkey had cooperated in the first Gulf War, and it was hoped the promise of six billion dollars in aid would inspire a similarly friendly attitude the second time around; thus planners had assumed a significant portion of American troops would enter Iraq, as I was doing, from the north. Barely three weeks before the invasion, however, in what may have proved to be a blessing in disguise for the American effort—the terms of one American offer would have allowed Turkish troops into northern Iraq, which might well have ignited a separate Turkish-Kurdish conflict there—Turkey's Grand National Assembly voted against allowing the Fourth Infantry Division passage through Turkey into Iraq.

I was traveling with Peter Galbraith, a frequent visitor to Iraq and the Kurdistan region in particular, and his son Andrew. Galbraith, a lawyer by training and a former U.S. ambassador to Croatia, who had advised the Kurds during the negotiations on the Transitional Authority Law (TAL), which would describe a legal framework for relations between Iraq's different religious and ethnic groups and regions until the writing of a constitution. He had been in Iraq during the Kurdish uprising in 1991 and, while fleeing across the Tigris into Syria, was nearly captured by Saddam's forces. He had done much to document and publicize Saddam's attacks upon Kurdish cities and his systematic destruction of Kurdish villages through displacement, rape, and murder. Many considered him an honorary Kurd.

Overcrowded and muddy from a morning rain, the border was expected to close in forty-eight hours due to election security procedures, and people of all sorts were rushing to get in or out. For our taxi driver the fare represented a good payday, and the danger across the border had nothing to do with him. Clearly familiar with the process, he made a series of stops at anonymous office buildings into which he took our passports. Our final stop before starting procedures with Turkish officials was at a gas station that specialized in siphoning off gas from taxis. Having sold their gas at a premium in Turkey, the drivers would get a full tank at cheaper prices on the other side of the border.

Standing in puddles of gasoline, with cigarettes hanging from the corners of their mouths, the attendants lined up each waiting car, propped up one tire, and siphoned the tank until the empty light flashed on the dashboard. An old man wandered in front of our car and flicked his ash near half-empty gasoline barrels. It flitted off in a gust of wind that failed to clear the fumes around the car. The attendants paid the man no mind; I bolted from the car to a dirt hill some twenty yards off. My reaction quickly became a bit of comic relief for those around the station. In a tableau of the absurd—cars awkwardly half-aloft, gas flowing out of full tanks into barrels, old men flirting with self-immolation, young men interrupting prayer to answer cell phones—acting in what seemed to me a reasonable manner, I had made myself look foolish to the locals. I was learning to be a guest here, not simply relinquishing control but adapting.

On this day, the Kurds also disappeared with our passports, but they offered us tea and food while we waited. The courtesy was not incidental. Some six weeks later, in Baghdad, I was talking to a South African private security contractor about the differences between that city and the Kurdish city of Arbil. "We're the dogs here [Iraq]. I know that," he said of hired bodyguards, "but in Arbil, when we visit an office with a client, they bring tea to our vehicles or positions." Arbil is many things that Baghdad is not, but considering his profession one might have expected the South African to note the relative safety as the foremost distinction. "People on the street here," he said of Kurdistan with a sense of awe born of having been in Baghdad too long, "will actually look at you for a second, even smile sometimes." After four hours in a cramped, smoke-filled taxi, a brief stop at an explosives dump disguised as a gas station, and the studied discourtesies of Turkish border officials, I did not need to visit Baghdad to appreciate Kurdish hospitality.

No proper introduction to the people, nineteenth- and twentieth-century colonial writers seem to concur, could omit to mention it. In his enduring memoir *Road Through Kurdistan*, published in 1937, Archibald Milne Hamilton, a New Zealander building a British road through the region, remarked on the "sacred obligation" of hospitality in Kurdistan. "A Kurdish host always likes to know when he should expect guests, that he may have food ready, and offer the best that he may provide."[1] Kurdish history is rife with war, politicking, and displacement. Many here have memories of long marches and periods of extreme deprivation, yet the culture cherishes the enjoyment of food and the business of playing host. In the coming months, I would observe the same enthusiasm, whether my dinner companions were the future president of Iraq and the prime minister of Kurdistan, or students in roadside shanties or displaced Iranian Kurds in refugee camps. Whether seated on couches in elegant living rooms, or on worn Kurdish rugs on the floors of bullet-ridden one-story concrete blocks some called home, long conversations were the rule preceding and following meals. On picnics in the foothills outside Mosul or in the mountains on the Iranian border, men would retreat from lunch to gossip, smoke, and play a game like bowling with rocks, while the women cleared plates and prepared tea and talked among themselves.

Having crossed the border, we were left to wait at a government compound that also served as an immigration center. From a small kitchen in a space shared with two holes—the bathroom—there emerged a guard in sandals who must have doubled as the compound's chef. For the three of us he brought out food enough for thirteen. Three large bowls of white rice; a pile of flat bread the diameter of a large pizza, stacked six inches high; peppers and tomatoes stuffed with boiled meat; freshly cooked kebabs. A stew of white beans and shredded chicken was for lack of space placed atop the kebabs. Dropped dismissively on the table as well were a couple heads of lettuce, fistfuls of spring onions, and a half dozen sliced tomatoes. Hamilton had been similarly overwhelmed: "On another tray are many dishes, of deliciously seasoned stews of vegetables and fruits and the choicest flesh of gamebirds and lambs—the latter having been specially killed for us." On this day, nothing had been killed in our honor, but a can of spaghetti, a gesture of understanding toward the Western palate, was offered as a side dish. Refilled water bottles were added for the sake of presentation.

On either side of the border, as far as one could see, Turkish and Iraqi truck drivers were also taking their lunch or afternoon tea. They did not have kebabs, but probably a cold version of the white bean stew and certainly the flat bread, which was made differently, I would learn, in each Kurdish city. Instead of dining on plastic tables as we were, the drivers ate on aluminum doors that folded down on hinges from the sides of the oil tankers. Our trip across the border from Diyarbakir had taken five hours. The trip from Zakho, the first real town beyond the border, to Arbil would take another four. An oil truck driver making the round-trip from a refinery in Turkey to northern Iraq and then back to Turkey, with a stop somewhere near Kirkuk to pick up crude, could take anywhere from three weeks to two months, with most of the time spent waiting.

Uphill and down, stretching over the plains, Turkish and Iraqi oil trucks stood in line. For the drivers in Silopi, on the Turkish side of the border, the most dangerous part of the job lay ahead. Scores of drivers, from as far away as China and as near as Egypt, had been kidnapped since the beginning of the war. Many had been killed. American truck drivers contracting with coalition forces traveled in guarded convoys and were also paid hand-somely for the risk. A Turkish driver down from Ankara would drive by himself, perhaps with an old pistol on the seat beside him. This afternoon, however, boredom, not danger, was the order of the day, as cabs sat empty and drivers lingered, eating around their trucks or on blankets by the side of the road. The small truck cabs were old and dusty, with the company's name or country of origin painted on the side in letters now chipping and peeling. Some men chatted with friends, some rolled dice on makeshift tables, and others simply sat on their haunches watch-ing nothing go by.

In places, the wait lines diverted into parking lots the size of football stadiums where trucks by the thousands were packed side by side. The scene resulted from one of those economies peculiar to war, such as Joseph Heller captured so well in *Catch-22*.

In Heller's mordant satire of the Second World War, Milo Minderbinder achieves notoriety and riches by buying high and selling low, thanks to the often peculiar constructs of wartime economies. At the end of January, gasoline was selling for around one dollar per liter in Turkey, while across the border in Iraqi Kurdistan, prices had settled at around ten cents per liter. But Turkish and Iraqi oil truck drivers had discovered that, via the black market and government subsidies, one could make a significant profit importing refined oil into Iraq and then illegally exporting that same refined oil. The trucks waiting to leave Iraqi Kurdistan were symptoms of a country plagued by violence and organized crime. For the better part of 2005, pipelines from the northern oil fields around Kirkuk were shut down, so all exporting of crude oil was done by truck. By September of that year, a new system involving extensive tribal security and unannounced openings and closings of the pipeline was allowing five million barrels of crude per month to flow out into Turkey—a mere fraction of Kirkuk's production capacity of nearly a million barrels a day. There was thus plenty of work for daring truck drivers.[2] The trucks carried crude into Turkey, to be refined in Turkish refineries and then imported back into Iraq. Iraq was in effect outsourcing the refining process of its own most valuable natural substance. According to former finance minister Ali A. Allawi, Iraq was consuming 20 million liters of gasoline per day in mid-2004 but producing only 12 million. With demand increasing and refinery capacity stagnant, Iraq would spend upward of $6 billion financing petroleum product imports in 2005.[3]

Having finished lunch, we sped south by the bored and restless truckers, in a convoy of four white Land Cruisers—two of them carrying a guard of eight Kurdish soldiers—doing sixty when no other vehicle on that street could even move, heading south away from the ark's supposed resting spot, past checkpoints as night fell, just north of Nineveh, where Jonah traveled after emerging from three days and nights in the belly of a great fish, downward closer to the tomb of Daniel in Kirkuk and that of the Shia martyr Ali in Najaf. For the first fifteen miles after we crossed the border, two pickup trucks with mounted machine guns escorted us through a series of mountain passes. En route to Arbil, we passed forty-five miles north of the provincial capital Mosul and cleared at least a dozen checkpoints. Despite the relative safety compared with central and western Iraq, it seemed like a war zone. We passed the four-hour drive with a mix tape of Kurdish, Iraqi, and Lebanese pop music on continuous loop.

At its worst, Oxford University can be a playpen for would-be politicians. At its best, it provides ambitious young men and women the opportunity to share ideas and connect with many of the world's preeminent thinkers and leaders. It was at Oxford in 2003 that I forged the friendships and ideas that led me to Kurdistan. It was through these friends that I would meet Peter Galbraith and then come to Iraq. By the beginning of 2005, the success of the spring 2003 march on Baghdad was fading in relevance in the face of a strengthening insurgency. Mosul had been lost, two battles fought for Falluja, and the Mahdi Army of Muqtada al-Sadr had risen in Baghdad and the south. But it was in distant pubs and gardens and seminar rooms, far from Iraq and far from Washington, in conversations with people from across the world, that I first began to think in earnest about the relationship between America and the world. It was a post–September 11th milieu—with the inevitable focus on cultural misunderstanding, religion and democracy, and security. I was admittedly much closer to the abstract, lofty ideas and partisanship that had created America's venture in Iraq than I was to the sand and violence within the country itself.

A stable democratic Iraq, the expansion of openness in the Middle East, and increased international goodwill toward the U.S.: these were all things, I believed, that would be good for

America. That a successful democratic Iraq would be a win-win situation for both Americans and Iraqis seemed a rather straightforward and simple truth. Not so simple, on the other hand, were the questions about how a nation historically ambivalent with regards to international entanglements might succeed in encouraging democracy, or, more immediately, how the violent tension between the West and parts of the Islamic world had arisen in the first place, and whether American intervention in these societies could possibly make things better.

In answer to a most basic question asked by many Americans on the morning of September 11, "Why do they hate us?" the influential scholar Bernard Lewis identified in contemporary Islam a political inclination that extremists had learned to exploit. Islam, according to Lewis, is a faith in which religion, politics, and society are historically and doctrinally more intertwined than in the Jewish or Christian traditions. In this view, there are in Islam tendencies which in the context of some cultures create a vulnerability to the seductions of fundamentalism and extremist political sentiment. This position, roughly generalized, suggests that whether the critical factor is described as a lack of societal openness to the free exchange of ideas or the want of a Protestant-style reformation of the faith, the realities underlying tension with the West are endemic to Islam. Similarly, the 9/11 Commission identified an age-old and "perverted" strand of Islam, which draws "on a long tradition of extreme intolerance within a minority strain of Islam that does not distinguish politics from religion, and distorts both."[4]

A contrary understanding places ultimate responsibility for this "minority strain" and the conflict in the Middle East today with the West and its history of inflammatory, ill-informed relations with the region, as well as with Afghanistan. This approach, whose advocates include Noam Chomsky and Tariq Ali, sees in the American response to Cold War crises in Israel, Afghanistan, and parts of Africa the undeniable seeds of Al Qaeda as well as less virulent manifestations of anti-Americanism. Mahmood Mamdani offers an incisive summary of this view in *Good Muslim, Bad Muslim: America, the Cold War, and the Roots of Terror:*

> The Islamic terror that we are witnessing today is more a mutation than an outgrowth of Islamic history, the result of a triple confluence: ideological, organizational, and political. The ideological element was the product of an encounter between Islamic intellectuals (Mawdudi, Qutb) and different Marxist-Leninist ideals that embraced armed struggle in the postwar period. The organizational element was a direct consequence of the American decision to organize the Afghan jihad as a quasi-private international crusade. The political element is a consequence of the demonization of Islam and its equation with terrorism, a tendency that emerged after the Cold War and gathered steam after 9/11.

Rather than regarding fundamentalism as growing inevitably out of Islam or Arab society, such a view holds that the misdeeds and miscalculations of governments past have come back to haunt the United States and its allies in the present. Even the nonpartisan 9/11 Commission recognized that foreign policy influences America's image abroad: "America's foreign policy choices have consequences. Right or wrong, it is simply a fact that American policy regarding the Israeli-Palestinian conflict and American actions in Iraq are dominant staples of popular commentary across the Arab and Muslim world." However, the report stops short of criticizing that policy per se, continuing: "That does not mean U.S. choices have been wrong."[5]

Whether one prefers to locate the causes for the tension between parts of Western culture and parts of Middle Eastern culture primarily on one side of the divide or the other, it has seemed useful to many commentators to sort the world and its ideas into "modern" and "pre-modern." True, this categorizing is more typical of those who regard the refusal of modernity as a symptom of Islamic civilization. But oddly enough, it was T. S. Eliot, champion par excellence of the West and its literary canon, modernist poet and religious reactionary, who provided the modern West its locus classicus on the evils of modernity, particularly as exemplified in the ascendance of certain extremist ideologies. In his 1939 essay "The Idea of a Christian Society," Eliot wrote:

> What we are seeking is not a programme for a party, but a way of life for a people: it is this which totalitarianism has sought to revive, and partly to impose by force upon its peoples. Our choice is not between one abstract form and another, but between a pagan, and necessarily stunted culture, and a religious, and necessarily imperfect culture.

Eliot believed that religion should inform every aspect of life, furnishing not a bedrock for earthly affairs but the soil, an all-encompassing, nurturing presence. And not unlike the totalitarian governments that proliferated in Europe at the time, Eliot—though he preferred Christian metaphysics to the triumph of the will—believed that the good life demands an overarching social structure more than any blessing of democracy and its associated freedoms. He continued:

> And it does not require a Christian attitude to perceive that the modern system of society has a great deal in it that is inherently bad . . . I confine myself therefore to the assertion, which I think few will dispute, that a great deal of the machinery of modern life is merely a sanction for un-Christian aims, that it is not only hostile to the conscious pursuit of the Christian life in the world by the few, but to the maintenance of any Christian society *of* the world.

As Eliot's pronouncement and recent European history make clear, an anxiety bred of modernity's commitment to materialism and individualism is hardly unique to contemporary Islam. And it is good to remember that the fascisms of Germany, Spain, and Italy, however different, were entirely Western in origin and formed partly in reaction to similar problems posed by modernity. Adolf Hitler may have been a killer with modern means and an adept deployer of modern propaganda techniques, but in his attempts to create a uniform and irrational sensibility among the German people, in essence to destroy individual identity, he was thoroughly antimodern. Like his fellow fascists, he played to fears of change and dislocation, nostalgically promising a return to an age when one's identity was secure and doubt nonexistent.[6]

In this sense, extreme versions of Islam today roughly resemble fascisms of the past: they offer seemingly simple solutions and explanations to the complicated problems poised by a changing world. The individual relinquishes all responsibility save faith and allegiance in exchange for an absolute metaphysical and social order. *The 9/11 Commission Report* on bin Laden's attraction: "He appeals to people disoriented by cyclonic change as they confront modernity and globalization." It continues: "For those yearning for a lost sense of order in an older, more tranquil world, offers his 'Caliphate' as an imagined alternative to today's uncertainty."[7] He calls his followers not to refuse the temptations of modernity but rather to evade its uncertainties and discomforts by clinging to tradition, seeking its illusory protection.

The commission's report details the elements of this uncertainty: lack of economic opportunity, illiteracy, political corruption, and social disenfranchisement. Whether these conditions are primarily the fruit of Islamic doctrine or the unintended consequences of Western malfeasance and ineptitude, or neither, has little bearing on the fact that they exist. Unless we are prepared to isolate the parts of the world called "modern" from those called "premodern," we must strive for integration, respect, and mutual coexistence, all of which depend on the discovery of an attractive alternative to extremist panaceas. One night after arriving in Iraq, I met an American soldier based in Mosul, to whom I explained my job at the university. We were, he noted, part of the same effort. He continued, "That's a big decision you've made. Can't be many volunteering to do that." A kind word, much appreciated, from one who had himself made a bigger decision to be there—until he walked away, adding with a chuckle: "There are some bad boys here who would love to get a hold of you."

True enough, the contending ideas must originate not with foreign intellectuals, but from within the society in need of change. As Mamdani argues, what the Islamic world needs is not imported modernity but sensitivity to "the emergence of an Islamic modernity, arising from processes within Islamic societies." Still, there must be appropriate and useful ways for those of us outside that society to support reformers and modernizers in it. We must first and foremost establish trust in our good intentions. Often the credibility of the small discrete act exceeds that of the grand gesture.

Mine is the generation of both Google and the wars in Iraq and Afghanistan. It is terribly fond of consumption and not shy of service. It is a generation for whom the end result of the Cold War was never really in doubt, who enjoyed relatively peaceful teenage years, and then matured into adulthood facing a new war that very few of us could understand. My contemporaries have helped, with their creativity and ingenuity, to usher in an information revolution to rival the industrial one; they have also, through discipline and force, helped usher out a dictator and topple governments. For most of us, our role in such grand changes seems small, even invisible—accomplished at a desk, in a cubicle, in a mess hall, in a turret. There are, of course, many struggles and efforts to be joined and contribution comes in an infinite multiplicity of forms, most of them measured in inches, and from all over the world.

Among the more obvious things Americans can do is teach English. Whether the enterprise seems imperialist or not, English is, and will be for the foreseeable future, the language of globalized modernity. Yet upon my arrival in the city of Arbil, there was not a single native speaker of American English teaching the language anywhere in the city. Nor did any of the schools or universities have teachers with backgrounds in American history.

That is what I was doing there. English—whether it travels via Shakespeare, anti-imperialists like Gandhi and Nehru, or anonymous teachers—is one of the West's great exports; it is something I could offer. And history can offer an honest way to talk about the American nation abroad.

I was to try my hand at teaching both—though first, I was told, I should try to get a gun.

3. The First Day of Class:
History in the Present

"WHAT kind of weapon are you going to carry?"

The question, asked by an aide of an American general a week before the start of classes, seemed a fair one. "Seriously," the general's bodyguard echoed, "get yourself a gun, some sort of gun." A translator from Baghdad chimed in just to make sure that I did not miss the point. "I'm sure the Ministry of Interior will give you one. Just ask them for a pistol or something."

Earlier in the week I had eaten dinner with, among others, Qubad Talabani and a friend of his, who directed the Iraq operations of a prominent British private security firm. Impressive and cosmopolitan in his own right, Qubad was the son of the future Iraqi president Jalal Talabani and therefore a target.

"If I were you," Qubad told me, "I'd have an armored car, with a second car of bodyguards following."

The British security official, well groomed, well spoken, was down to his signet ring a Central Casting paragon of correctness; he could have prospered in a century past. He had been in Iraq for nearly two years and his dinner talk on this night rarely tended toward politics. His immediate concern seemed to be adventure. He was in the process of importing two kayaks so he could navigate down the Tigris and was heading off the next day for a mountain-bike trip, on which he invited me to tag along. I need not worry, he added, he could provide me with a bike, and the two jeeploads of armed guards would surely be sufficient for both of us. Quintessentially British though the security official was, Robert Duvall in *Apocalypse Now,* surfboard and all, comes to mind. It was only after hearing him tell of a heli-ski trip he'd planned in the mountains of northern Iraq—a perfectly pleasant jaunt vetoed by an American general—that I could get him to focus on the question of security in Arbil, Iraqi Kurdistan's largest city.

"Our clients move in armored vehicles," he noted. "They have two professionals in the car with them and four peshmerga [Kurdish militia members] in a follow car."

"I must say," he continued, "I think things are getting worse there. It's the road between Kirkuk and Mosul. I keep waiting to hear that we have lost somebody. It is only a matter of time, really."

"I'd teach with a bodyguard on each shoulder," he added. "Have them with you all the time, two teams on seven-day shifts. It may be uncomfortable, but you'll get used to it."

Here it was early 2005; the American invasion of Iraq was nearing its second anniversary, the first national election since the fall of Saddam was taking place, and nobody could or would give me a precise explanation of the security situation except to say that even in the Kurdish areas, thought by outsiders to be secure, Iraq was dangerous. Arbil is in the north, about ninety minutes east of Mosul and two hours northwest of Kirkuk by car. It is a sprawling city of dust and concrete, more scarred by Saddam's violence and civil wars than by the recent American actions and the ensuing insurgency. Since the rise of insurgency violence, it had taken on some of the familiar physical character- istics of a city under siege and threatened with shootings, car bombs, and suicide bombings. Blast walls were proliferating; checkpoints were commonplace.

The American's advice had been the most self-reliant. "Nobody can protect you better than yourself."

The Kurd's had been the most philosophical: "If someone is willing to blow themselves up to get you, well, you can't really do anything about that."

As for the Brit, he reiterated his invitation to go mountain biking.

I had yet to be provided guards when I was given the modern history class for third- and fourth-year students in the College of Arts, with the option to teach American history as long as discussion of the Middle East occurred as well. "Just teach a little about America maybe, Europe if you want, and the Middle East," the well-dressed and affable head of the department had advised casually, inviting me to share some tea and conversation about history in his office. My group was in the "Historical Texts" division of the department, he informed me, meaning that class was to be structured around historical documents or readings that would be practiced at home and read aloud in class. The readings were to be in English, as were the classroom lectures—this was not an exception made on my account but rather the norm. After years of such learning—in an atmosphere more akin to an SAT prep class than any idealized form of a university lecture hall—the students could read aloud and write exams from memory in reasonably good English, but none apparently could speak the language well or understand it above the level of basic conversation.

Neither Guevara, a broad-shouldered, slightly chubby, often unshaven, and usually gregarious young man who sat in the front row, nor Bayan, a wiry and energetic though unforthcoming young woman who always sat flanked by her two best friends, had ever conversed in English with a native speaker. This was an intriguing novelty, and so from the first day of lecture, as on every other day, the foremost problem was not with attendance or attention, but with convincing the students that discussing American history could be more interesting than idly chatting with an American. Bayan and friends, the close-knit trio who rarely missed a class and always listened politely, were often too shy to ask questions or even read aloud, but they insisted on taking group photographs with me after class. By contrast, Azad, a skinny guy, bearded and almost always dressed in black sweaters and slacks, obsessively brought every discussion around to the tangled skeins of Islam, America, and the Middle East. He approached the knotty question with the restless need to know of one who felt his life might be affected in practical ways by the answers—rather as many Americans have begun to read obsessively about the same subjects after decades of relative indifference. Never mind about Thomas Jefferson and the Declaration of Independence; George W. Bush's declarations were the ones in most urgent need of parsing.

Leaving aside the challenges of language and the students' alternative interests, I was well aware of some inherent flaws in my effort. Continuity and trust are important elements of education. My sudden appearance had thrown the former out the window, and I had only one term before summer break to develop the latter. Furthermore, one of the historian's greatest responsibilities to his or her students, as well as to the material, is a conscious dedication to impartiality and fairness. This is one of history's great challenges in the best of circumstances. But an American abroad, especially in Iraq, could easily lose perspective about America, whether in the country's favor or not. It was up to me to ensure that my history class never became an exercise in triumphalism or an occasion for America-bashing. In the end, my bona fides would have to be my own education as well as my presence as an American in no official capacity. In addition, I was the only one willing to take the job. It was me or it was no American history, no American interlocutor at all. In a city where American products, from Pepsi to movies and music, were pouring in, in a country where American troops had recently deposed a dictator and were patrolling the streets, the choice of ignorance could be a dangerous one. Americans were already in Iraq; the context furnished by American history, in whatever imperfect form, could be more than relevant.

Postconflict educational and cultural exchanges are nothing new in the modern world; nor are the attendant complications. When the British assumed the mandate in Iraq following World War I, they instituted public education with as much concern for the potential dangers posed by political consciousness stoked by communism as for the potential benefits. Before then, individual Americans had long been in the region as missionaries and educators, establishing in 1866, for example, the Syrian Protestant College in Beirut, which would later become the well-respected American University in Beirut.[1] Beyond the Middle East, such exchanges were vital to bridging the Cold War divide after 1945. In describing the founding of institutions like UNESCO (United Nations Educational, Scientific, and Cultural Organization), the Harvard historian Akira Iriye notes: "The widespread belief was that not just by spreading Western values or transferring Western technology to the East, but also by bringing the two perspectives together, would it become possible for the countries of the world to build a solid basis for international order."[2] Implementation of this philosophy is never as simple in practice as in principle. Diplomacy bumps up against historical methodology.

There is a particular conundrum about teaching one's national history abroad—finding the fine line where intellectual honesty and nationalist interests overlap, without compromising one or subverting the other. The effort is limited and made more difficult by a lack of national consensus. Our often strident disagreement over issues at home, our sometimes vocal criticism of the government or of individual parties, nevertheless takes place within a set of shared principles, a general philosophy upon which most Americans agree. Jefferson articulated those ideas simply and elegantly, and we all continue to believe axiomatically in the rights to life, liberty, and the pursuit of happiness. Most Americans also believe in God and a better life after this one, yet they work no less earnestly to improve their place in our world. Much of what allows our national coherence despite our internal disagreements goes unspoken most of the time. But we assume at our peril that our notions of the individual in society resonate intuitively with other cultures.

I would have to balance the historian's essential skepticism with a somewhat natural urge to show America in a not unfavorable light. While history is no longer considered in many academic circles to be an exercise in objectivity, evidence is not meant to be forced into any preexisting story or narrative. The historian should begin with an open-ended question. As the historian Joyce Appleby has observed, the writing of one's own nation's history is

> different from other historical work, for with it, a relatively open-ended scholarly inquiry collides with the vigilant censor of national self-interest and the group pressure of celebratory self-fashioning. And when this happens, historians are made acutely aware that they are also citizens who believe that what their country represents is integrally connected to what one thinks the country has done in the past.[3]

To do history is inevitably to confront awkward as well as more edifying truths.

.   .   .

Finally, I decided that rather than run from this problem, the class would meet it head-on. Nations make mistakes. Whatever their intentions, they err, sometimes horribly, as even their heroes allow. In the eighteenth century, George Washington saw the destruction of the American Indian peoples, and its consequences, in perspective. Oppression of the Indians and confiscation of their lands would, according to the first president, "stain the character of a nation." In his memoirs, near the end of the nineteenth century, Ulysses S. Grant referred to the Civil War as a moral reckoning or penance for the injustice of the Mexican-American War. Though George W. Bush declared that he could think of no mistake he had made in his first term, many of the nation's leaders in the past century, from Franklin D. Roosevelt to Robert McNamara, have been moved to publicly acknowledge their mistakes and those of the country. The mea culpa has always served less as contrition and more as a rededication to the principles for which America stands. We are not unerringly a country of the free with a history of freedom, but one that is ever struggling to move closer to a full and authentic realization of its ideals. An American historian recently pointed out that perhaps no other people in history have had more opportunity, and thus more opportunity to fail, than Americans. The idea of America is less about where you have been or where you are than about where you can go. To be sure, we have suffered through the imperial paradox that plagued the British in the nineteenth and twentieth centuries: that of an avowedly democratic country with millions of disenfranchised subjects. America's strength has always been the compulsive return to founding principles in making sense of our course.

With this in mind, I chose texts from among both the canonical voices of America's founding as well as the once marginal voices we have come to revere, voices of protest whose call for change was couched more or less explicitly in the language of founding principles. We would read Martin Luther King Jr. and Langston Hughes as well as Jefferson and Madison. Zora Neale Hurston and Bob Dylan would also be heard in this classroom. We would discuss the most American of revolutionaries, not only those who first set our course but those too who in various forms had urged us in our way back toward it, among them Walt Whitman, Elvis Presley, and Muhammad Ali.

On the morning of my first class, I arrived fifteen minutes early at the history department office. As if I had been there for years, an elderly clerk gave me the class roll and offered me tea before returning to his papers, unable to conceal a smirk of amusement at my being there. There were several absentees that first day, but the class's ranks had nevertheless swelled beyond the number of those enrolled. History students had brought friends, friends had brought curious acquaintances, and with all the seats filled, some were standing against the wall in the back. I apparently was something to see, and in greeting the class in Kurdish—*"Choni, boshi,"* hello, how are you—I seemed not to disappoint. Smiles, laughs, and English "hellos" were returned. Despite the obvious incongruity of the situation, there was nevertheless an air of seriousness in the classroom. While I may have been a curiosity, they treated me with respect and engaged with that day's lesson without hesitation.

And where better to begin the class?

We hold these truths to be self-evident, that all men are created equal, that they are endowed by their Creator with certain unalienable Rights, that among these are Life, Liberty and the pursuit of Happiness.

Not a single student in the class had ever heard these words. Jefferson's words are not simply the poetic beginning of the United States, but an expression of ideas whose influence has stretched across continents and centuries.° Ho Chi Minh, having arrived at Ba Dinh Square in Hanoi on September 2, 1945, had read them aloud from the new Vietnamese Declaration of Independence. And though the ideas themselves may have reached Arbil, this articulation of them had not. One student recognized the phrases as having to do with America but had never heard them read aloud. An adventurous girl in the second row offered to read the day's second "historical text," a section of Martin Luther King's "Letter from a Birmingham Jail."[5]

Before the Pilgrims landed at Plymouth, we were here.

I interrupted to ask whether any in the class had heard of Dr. King, and all shook their heads with certainty. Then a middle-aged male student modestly raised his hand to pose a question to my translator, who then turned to me and asked: "The student is confused. First, he's not sure that you're right. He says that Martin Luther was German, not American. Second, he says he thought America had no royalty." Almost everyone in the class knew of the great Protestant reformer, but practically no one had heard of the great reformer of the civil rights movement.

Far from Europe, I explained, King had penned these words from a prison cell in the state of Alabama. I told of how, in the five years before King's arrival in 1963 to protest segregation in the city, eighteen black churches and homes had been burned there. His arrest came on April 12, Good Friday, I told the class, and he spent the next eight days in prison, initially in solitary confinement. One of the nation's most profound meditations on

°A complete translation of the document was available by September 1776. Newspapers and journals in Italy and Switzerland followed with Italian and German translations over the following months. The historian David Armitage tells us that Frederick Douglass specifically alluded to the Declaration some seventy-six years later: "The Declaration was known to the whole world and that world would judge America according to the document's standards."[4]

justice, equality, and religion was written from a prison cell in the margins of newspaper's and on scraps of paper smuggled to the prisoner.

Before the pen of Jefferson etched across the pages of history the majestic words of the Declaration of Independence, we were here. If the inexpressible cruelties of slavery could not stop us, the opposition we now face will surely fail. We will win our freedom because the sacred heritage of our nation and the eternal will of God are embodied in our echoing demands.

Through King, we had returned to the words of Jefferson. How did it come about that America had at its birth recognized the equality of men as "self-evident," only to find itself nearly two hundred years later still denying the rights and opportunities of equality to a large minority whose roots in America were as old as the nation itself? What dynamics had brought about this contradiction? The translator pressed the questions forward. While some students had a bit of background in American history, none had studied race relations or the evolution of civil rights in America. But understanding was immediate. Pawns of geopolitics in the 1970s, denied the right to speak their language in Turkey and areas of Iraq, hundreds of thousands of them killed during Saddam's systematic violence, Kurds understood only too well the experience of a people's subjugation. Although most in my classroom were slightly too young to remember the 1988 gassing of five thousand civilians in Halabja, over one hundred miles to the southeast of Arbil, the atrocity had been imprinted in their minds as they grew up, some of them in that very town.

Hands flew up in a flurry. Sarhang, a male student in the back row, focused on me intensely, looking for an instantaneous evaluation of his answer. "Because the whites felt that they were better, that the blacks were only slaves," he offered. No nods of agreement and none of the hands went down. Seeing no immediate approval in my eyes, other students sent their answers in different directions. It was admittedly a complicated question with complicated answers.

One student took an anthropological approach: "Because the whites, they were Europeans. The Europeans said that they were higher, they had more development than the Africans."

Another voice echoed that answer: "The whites had the European civilization that was the most important in America."

Calling upon a rough sense of history and a refined sense of power, they had gathered from the mention of slavery that appeals to cultural superiority and religion were the most likely bases for justifying that peculiar institution and its residue of rigid racial hierarchy. This was not, however, on their part or mine, an effort to draw parallels. Guevara insistently pointed out that the story of the Kurds in Iraq was not one of a minority denied rights but a people denied their nation. Nevertheless, Sarhang, Bayan, and several others had no difficulty guessing how minorities were denied their rights for most of America's history; at times they looked to their own people's experience for clues.

As I made my way up the stairs to the history building's second floor, many of the students would be gathered on the landing to see whether I was going to show up. Some huddled to gossip and others to exchange notes, but many were simply waiting to see whether that day was the day I would stop coming to the college. Americans have a reputation for doing great things in the Kurdish region of Iraq. We also have a history of disappearing at rather crucial moments. The anxiety of the third- and fourth-year history students that I might give up and return home without telling them, I would discover over the course of the term, was rooted not as much in my nationality as in theirs. This generation's experience of its place in the world had been dramatically different from that of their parents. Many did not speak Arabic and their hopes and ambitions had matured during the years of autonomy after the first Gulf War, as opposed to the decades under Saddam's direct rule. The years of autonomy and isolation had bred a guarded optimism: things might be getting better, but they might, just as unpredictably, get worse—or, to the great frustration of the youth, simply stay the same. They were, in short, always waiting for the other shoe to fall. There was, however, genuine openness. At humorous moments in class, they would laugh without hesitation or restraint. Men like Sarhang and women like Bayan were never discouraged by their peers from expressing opinions. So far as I saw, nobody ever challenged or grew impatient with Azad's incessant inquisitiveness about Islam and Christianity. In fact, it was not until the final day of class that I saw disagreement turn uncivil—and that dispute would concern an attack not on a fellow classmate, but upon me.

In a whirlwind of English and Kurdish, we moved with broad strokes through America's founding ideals as well as the "peculiar institution's" ugly history, working steadily toward the Civil War. Drawing maps of the expanding United States with faded markers, I pointed out St. Louis and Boston. Students asked about New York City and Washington, D.C. One wanted to know the location of Las Vegas. The red line of the western border moved almost daily, blue and green stripes delineating the coming divide between North and South. The classroom in which I taught had a single whiteboard covered in faded blue characters, both Arabic and Kurdish, which a previous lecturer had scribbled without bothering to notice that he was using a permanent pen. The room had no blinds and many of its forty-five or so desks were falling apart. Trash was picked up only a couple of times a week and scraps of paper and other rubbish collected in the corners of the room.

.   .   .

It was the third week of class when we reached the Civil War—a point in American history when beginnings and endings coincided, when things began to get better by getting much worse. "How," I asked the class, "might a social and economic order so important to much of the country come to an end?" It had been my experience that when called on students sometimes needed some time to work through their thoughts out loud, sometimes offering rather complicated analyses at first and answering the question directly only in the concluding summaries. This time, however, only one student raised his hand and the answer was as short as it was simple.

"Abraham Lincoln. Because Abraham Lincoln said so."

As one of the day's readings made clear, Frederick Douglass had offered an entirely different answer nearly one hundred and fifty years before, "We were not saved by the captain, but by the crew. We are not saved by Abraham Lincoln, but by the power behind the throne." Teaching the Civil War and its causes, I admitted to the class, is complicated by continuing disagreement in America about its causes and its legacy, and the degree to which it haunts our national psyche not only as our great epic but as the near-fatal wound that caused the greatest national self-examination since the founding days. Three class periods were, needless to say, utterly insufficient for exploring the roots and terrible nature of the War Between the States, but those days did provide a context for what might have been an otherwise abstract discussion of the American political system and its protection of states' rights from the federal government. They also furnished a degree of immediacy and relevance. For while in America the idea of civil war has been saturated with sentimentalizing tones of blue and gray feeding the bottomless appetite of history buffs, questions of civil war, federalism, and minority rights were part of the inescapable here and now in Iraq, key concepts attached to both hope and pessimism regarding the country's future. For the aggressively pro-independence among the Kurds, who saw in Saddam's ouster the prospect of a truly independent homeland, the words bespoke the gamut of possible relationships, from violent to symbiotic, with the rest of Iraq. Civil war meant young men and money spent fighting southward, while federalism and minority rights meant being part of federal Iraq and perhaps an Arab-dominated one at that.

The week's final historical text was the Thirteenth Amendment. Bayan's shy friend Jiyan—whose name means, literally, "freedom"—struggled with the first clause but persisted.[6]

Neither slavery nor involuntary servitude, except as a punishment for crime whereof the party shall have been duly convicted, shall exist within the United States, or any place subject to their jurisdiction.

Once again class had run beyond its scheduled period, and as the students packed up to leave, I asked if there were any remaining questions. Like students anywhere, most sat silently clutching their bags and notebooks, poised to bolt. Azad, excited and insatiably inquisitive as usual, raised his hand.

"Why did not the religious people note that Jesus didn't have slaves? Why did not they say that Jesus would say no to slaves?"

A normally rather moderate student named Mohammed jumped in with equal fervor: "Yes, but what was the Christian religion saying?"

We had talked at some length about religion's role in nineteenth-century America, and I had alluded to its importance in the civil rights movement. The frustrations of Mohammed and Azad were not with the history or how we were studying it, but with the implications America's history had for their preconceptions of modern Christianity. This was a class made up entirely of Sunni Muslims, who, although relaxed about their practices in many cases, still drew much of their identity from their religion, and imagined that everyone who professed a religion did likewise. In the coming months, we would stumble through repeated questions about Jews, America, and Israel—questions that, it seems, required more trust than we had yet developed. Still, even at this early point in the class, they were not at all shy in posing questions about Christianity. Perhaps it was because they had nothing to hide: while many of their opinions about Jews would fit rather neatly into conspiracy theories about vastly disproportionate influence and wealth, their inquiries about Christianity revealed a favorable, if monolithic, impression.

While my students could comprehend how Sunni insurgents would bomb Shia funerals and even mosques just sixty miles to the west in Mosul, they could not comprehend the idea that Christianity might be used to defend different sides of the same issue, as it had in the case of slavery (the Northern abolitionists versus Southern clergy who, citing Abrahamic precedent, argued for a kinder, gentler slavery) and would again during the civil rights movement. The students who broached the subject, and the many who sought me out after class, were disconcerted to learn of the Christian religion's own schisms and disagreements. Though they had heard of Martin Luther, they knew little of the difference in belief between Protestants and Catholics and there was no sense of the differences in belief within modern America, or between America and Europe. Christianity may have been the religion of the aggressors during the Crusades—Salahaddin (Saladin), for whom the university was named, was the Kurdish and Arab leader who had recaptured Jerusalem from the Europeans in 1187—it was also, as these Kurds saw it, the religion of liberators in the present. Although northern Iraq is home to tens of thousands of Christians, largely Assyrian and Chaldean, the religion is very much associated with

America and the West. The indigenous manifestations didn't figure in my students' minds. For while religion has become increasingly embroiled in American culture wars and internal politics, Mohammed and Azad understood Christianity as a simple good, a moderate faith that suffered none of the extremism or infighting that has plagued Islam. Osama bin Laden and other violent extremists, as they saw it, were blights upon their religion.

Especially when the issues verged on the personal, our discussions often continued out into halls and onto the small, unkempt lawns of the university's courtyards. For the most part, after we left class the students had much more to teach me than I had to teach them: When do the famous Kurdish mushrooms, the ones like truffles, start appearing in the bazaar? Spring. Where do most of the Failis, or Shia Kurds, live? Baghdad, though many live near the border with Iran. That day of discussing the role of religion in nineteenth-century America, a young female student stopped me outside and asked for a photograph. While smiling for the university's unofficial cameraman, she asked me in a shy and uncertain manner, "Don't you think blacks should have used Christianity as a point for freedom? Used the writings that show all are one. My understanding is Christianity says all humans are one, the same."

In January 1865, General William Tecumseh Sherman and Secretary of War Edwin Stanton met with twenty black ministers in Savannah, Georgia, to sound out their notions about the status of Georgia's freedmen. At black churches across the North, from Illinois to Connecticut, the Emancipation Proclamation was celebrated. Hymns praised both freedom and nationalism, folding the proclamation and the declaration "into one seamless story," in the words of the historian David Blight. And yet the hopes of the twentieth century's most famous minister would remain unfulfilled when he spoke these words almost exactly a century later.[7]

I have a dream that one day the state of Alabama, whose governor's lips are presently dripping with the words of interposition and nullification, will be transformed into a situation where little black boys and black girls will be able to join hands with little white boys and white girls and walk together as sisters and brothers . . . This is our hope. This is the faith with which I return to the South. With this faith we will be able to hew out of the mountain of despair a stone of hope. With this faith we will be able to transform the jangling discords of our nation into a beautiful symphony of brotherhood. With this faith we will be able to work together, to pray together, to struggle together, to go to jail together, to stand up for freedom together, knowing that we will be free one day.

I asked Sera, an attractive woman with large round eyes, who, contrary to common practice, wore little makeup on her unblemished face and no *hejab*, to repeat the final line: *With this faith we will be able to work together, to pray together, to struggle together, to go to jail together, to stand up for freedom together, knowing that we will be free one day.* How is it, I asked, that generations after the Thirteenth, Fourteenth, and Fifteenth Amendments were enacted, Martin Luther King Jr. could still be talking about being free "one day"—and had not yet abandoned the hope of moving forward "together"? What do you think happened, or did not happen, I asked the class, in the century between the Emancipation Proclamation and Dr. King's most famous speech?

Although some of my questions were met with blank stares or extended silences, this one drew immediate and extensive responses. The proffered hypotheses varied, but all of them bore the imprint of a people long disadvantaged—of a psychological and material understanding of what it meant to be second-class citizens.

"Many had no political power. The whites had all the political power," said a feisty older man in the back of the class.

"Blacks and some immigrants were second-class people, no support from power and no representation in power," echoed a student from the front.

One young woman saw a connection between such political status and education. "Some blacks maybe were illiterate and so could not voice their position or change politics."

One student overcame his obvious shyness to lead the conversation in another direction. "Many were economically backward," he said, using a term that would come back some weeks later in reference to the Middle East itself. "They had to work for free so had nothing to start with. No businesses." Perhaps it was not just politics, but the economic legacy of slavery as well. His posture eased as classmates nodded in approval.

With no background in the period, the class had again done remarkably well in surmising the elements of economic and political oppression coupled with violence and intimidation that minority groups, immigrants, and even women would face in America during the final decades of the nineteenth century. But we also spoke briefly of P. B. S. Pinchback, son of a Southern planter and his former slave, who became acting governor of Louisiana for thirty-five days in the early 1870s and later was a practicing lawyer. There were people and events whose notable Reconstruction-era successes embodied the greatest early hopes of those either born free or recently set free or who had just arrived in the "land of the free."

We moved slowly, without much discussion or question, through the failure of the nevertheless admirable Freedman's Bureau, the postwar system of sharecropping, and the "Black Codes." The class was familiar with the concept of segregation and quickly grasped the implications of the Jim Crow laws and the 1896 *Plessy v. Ferguson* decision that upheld the racial divide.

The lectures on segregation and lynching laid bare a tension that had been present in class from the beginning. If I was honest enough to discuss days when African Americans could be strung up from a tree and burned alive by fellow townsfolk, they surmised, perhaps I would also be honest in my characterization of American sins today. And so they ventured forth.

"I hear that Rice owns greatest oil company," one student insisted.

Even in the north, where Kurds welcomed American intervention as liberation, there was considerable attention given to America's oil interests in Iraq. The student could offer no names of companies or even a source for the story, but he was quite certain of its accuracy. I dismissed the notion that Rice had a hand in the oil business, but the class's reaction showed me how difficult it would be to prove that my nation's intentions were good when more sinister motives were so easily inferred.

"Maybe you are right," Hawza, Guevara's buddy and equal in force of opinion, stated. "America could have come about Saddam and about the democracy. But America is not going where the oil is not." Some legitimate counterevidence, such as American involvement in Bosnia or Kosovo, could not, it seemed, defeat the overwhelming circumstantial logic of an oil-hungry nation intervening in a country with one of the world's largest oil reserves.

"Do you think I get any oil for coming here?" I asked in half-mocking frustration.

The class laughed at the suggestion, and it became clear that Hawza's comments were informed less by a sense of America and her people than by notions of leaders in general. In his mind, it was not the American people who wanted oil, but Condoleezza Rice. Nearly twenty-five years of Baathist rule and ten years of semiautonomous isolation with limited development had produced in these students the sense of an absolute divide between rulers and the governed. The Kurdish prime minister, Nechirvan Barzani, and his uncle Massoud Barzani, might be widely admired and respected, but they lived in luxurious, secure, gated compounds high in the hills outside of Arbil.

Discussion moved from unanswerable questions of conspiracy to general ones more clearly related to the curriculum and having to do with America's image abroad. In a tone that began as accusatory but slowly warmed to sympathetic, Bashar, an intelligent and always well-prepared student, asked: "If racism is in America today, how can you come to the Middle East and tell the Middle East things to do?"

There is a long history of adversaries holding up a mirror to the American nation to show how the Land of the Free fails its own ideals even while pressing them upon other societies. In 1949, the Soviet Union received Paul Robeson as much to demonstrate how progressive communism was on the issue of race compared with America as to honor his achievement as singer, athlete, and statesman. During the Vietnam War, the North Vietnamese Army and Vietcong broadcast English-language accounts of racism and violence in America to black soldiers in the field.

"Do you think," Bashar asked, "that the racism makes it so America cannot do change in Syria or Lebanon?"

"Do our problems at home mean we can't have a voice abroad?" I asked in reply.

"I have good information on the election for George Bush and John Kerry," he answered, sitting up and leaning forward, proud of his sources. "The election it was good and fair. It is open. In America you criticize your president so it is open and that will help you."

I said nothing in response. We live in a world where a country is judged by more than its actions. In the age of satellite television and blogs, dictators and mullahs, image can affect perception as much as reality can. Here was a young man who had attempted to find out on his own some facts about America and its claims about freedom and democracy. His sources had led him to certainty about a favorable conclusion. They could just as easily have led him to the Bush administration's covert deployment of journalists, for instance, or to its counterproductive condemnation of the Dixie Chicks' dissent over the war. Thanks to the machinations of global media, relatively inconsequential misdeeds could be as harmful to America's reputation abroad as all the fanciful tales of oil grabs or Zionist plots. To give the deliberations of ordinary individuals a sounder foundation upon which to draw conclusions about us was one of my primary reasons for being in Iraq. But I had to marvel: from some ten thousand miles away and unaware of significant currents of American discontent with Washington, this young man had weighed American democracy and, guided more by intuition than hard fact, had found it essentially virtuous.

Democracy was still in its infancy in Iraq, even in Kurdistan, where a democratically elected legislature had been in place since 1992. Yet, as this young Kurd had understood, democracy is not an absolute, and unlike its formal trappings—assemblies and prime ministers—it is actually instituted by degrees. Bashar spoke out of some frustration with his society's still relatively small allowances or space for criticism of government and leaders. It was not that he, or anybody in the classroom, had anything particularly negative to say about Nechirvan, or then Iraqi prime minister Iyad Allawi (everybody here had something critical to say about Ahmed Chalabi). But in the putatively free press and other media, such as Kurdistan Television and Khabat (the newspaper that proclaimed itself, not without pride, the "organ of the KDP," the dominant political party), Bashar had simply never seen anything like open debate, let alone outright criticism. His endorsement of American democracy carried with it a hint of rebuke about the Iraqi version. In addition to legal restrictions on extreme criticism, or slander, of Kurdish politicians, there were also cultural ones—party loyalties in place for decades and tribal ones much older than that—and this young man had no cause to believe they would fall away anytime soon.

Bayan, my translator and co-teacher, struggled when I introduced the concept of lynching. Three times she asked me to repeat my explanation of the more than 4,500 recorded deaths, including at least 161 African Americans in 1892 alone, that took place in the American South between 1882 and 1960 as a result of mob violence. She believed something was being lost in translation—that the raw, lawless violence that was becoming a daily event in Iraq could not have taken place in the United States. To cover such a period in American history required a degree of confidence—confidence in some redemption to come and confidence that the students would be disciplined and open-minded enough to listen to the whole story. Had the nation not survived the problem of the "color line," what W. E. B. Du Bois called the "problem of the twentieth century," I would almost surely have been in no position, ethically or practically, even to be there teaching the course. America's authority as an example depends not on forgetting its darker moments but on how it struggles against them. So it would be in class as well. Had my students abandoned the endeavor or had the class been cancelled the day after we covered slavery, the disservice to their country and mine would have far outweighed any benefit. But, fortunately, just as history did not halt in its course, my students kept coming and so did I.

As always, we concluded with a reading in English. We had reached the end of Dr. King's most famous speech, and a young

woman crowded into a corner of the packed classroom mispro-
nounced her way through his stirring words. Please read it again,
I asked. This time she found a rhythm in language.

*So let freedom ring. From the prodigious hilltops of New
Hampshire, let freedom ring. From the mighty mountains of
New York, let freedom ring. From the heightening Alleghenies of
Pennsylvania, let freedom ring. But not only that; let freedom
ring from Stone Mountain of Georgia. Let freedom ring from
every hill and molehill of Mississippi. And when this happens,
when we let it ring, we will speed that day when all God's children, black men and white men, Jews and gentiles, Protestants
and Catholics, will be able to join hands and sing in the words of
the old Negro spiritual: Free at last, free at last. Thank God
Almighty, we're free at last.*

As the classroom emptied, an energetic young student, his
eyes bright, his body bent forward in apparent anticipation of
our exchange, waited for me outside. He grabbed me just by the
door and asked, "Why didn't blacks just go and form their own
country?"

My students doubted not just politicians and political institutions but the very project of Iraq itself. Why remain part of any
country where you are deemed less than a full citizen, especially
given a history of violence and oppression? Here was a historical
comparison, he suggested, that was worth pursuing.

4. Election Day in a Country Within a Country

My grandfather had a good sense of humor. He used to say he was born a Kurd, in a free country. Then the Ottomans arrived and said to my grandfather, "You're Ottoman," so he became Ottoman. At the fall of the Ottoman Empire, he became Turkish. The Turks left and he became a Kurd again in the kingdom of Sheikh Mahmoud, king of the Kurds. Then the British arrived, so my grandfather became a subject of His Gracious Majesty and even learned a few words of English.

The British invented Iraq, so my grandfather became Iraqi, but this new word, Iraq, always remained an enigma to him, and to his dying breath he was never proud of being Iraqi; nor was his son, my father."

—*Hiner Saleem*, My Father's Rifle

ON January 30, 2005, in cities once overrun by Alexander the Great and the Mongols, in towns extant since the Assyrians and the Medes, in villages that still bore the mark of Ottoman rule, Kurds went to vote in a country invented by the British and until recently was held together by a ruthless dictator.

Three days earlier, Abu Musab al-Zarqawi, Iraq's most infamous terrorist, had cast his own figurative vote against rule of the people. "We have declared a fierce war on this evil principle of democracy and those who follow this wrong ideology," the Jordanian born al-Zarqawi announced via a recording on an Islamist website. Unknown before the war, he had become a dominant force in the insurgency, striking dread throughout the country as Al Qaeda's man in Iraq. Al-Zarqawi condemned candidates as "demi-idols" and voters as "infidels." "Anyone who tries to help set up this system is a part of it." With daily violence around the country and especially in Baghdad's streets, al-Zarqawi's threats had substance. Understandably anxious candidates withheld their names and photos until the last minute, campaigning mainly by radio and television (interim prime minister Ayad Allawi advertised on Baghdad television almost twenty-four hours a day): personal appearances were extremely rare. Voter registration, too, was postponed in many places until the last minute, as was the announcement of polling station locations.

Optimistic Kurds, assuming greater than proportional representation, foresaw the Kurdish slate receiving 30 percent of the national vote. Since the 1970s, and particularly following the uprising of 1991, Kurdish politics had been dominated by two parties: the Kurdistan Democratic Party (KDP), a family affair led by Massoud Barzani, the son of the charismatic legend Mullah Mustafa—not a cleric, despite the title, but a peerless hero of armed nationalism; and the Patriotic Union of Kurdistan (PUK), an umbrella party led by Jalal Talabani, a larger-than-life figure in his own right and a formidable force in Kurdish politics for decades. (An Islamist party, a Communist party, and Assyrian and Turkomen parties have vied to capture the little remaining influence, patronage, and organizational resources.) For the purposes of this national election, however, the KDP and PUK had combined forces to form one ticket. Some complained that the curtailment of choice undermined the democratic spirit; others saw the cooperation as a sign of progress in Kurdish politics. In any case, showing a unified front greatly improved the electoral chances of the Kurds, and the turnout would prove substantial enough to send some of the best Kurdish politicians to Baghdad. First, however, the day's politics had to be conducted locally.

It snowed on election day. In Salahaddin, a secure mountainous village about an hour outside of Arbil, men in traditional Kurdish dress lingered after their turn at the ballot box, awaiting the arrival of Massoud Barzani and his nephew Nechirvan, who would soon be prime minister of Kurdistan. Nechirvan is billed by some as the future of Kurdish politics; he is a suave, modern-thinking politician who can talk in intimate terms about his country and its future while pouring Opus One and Johnny Walker Blue at parties for visiting journalists and former officials of Western governments. The dual capacity is well suited to the demands of Kurdish politics. The future of his party requires that he maintain down-home credibility, but in fact the fate of the Kurdish people has often been decided abroad—whether at the League of Nations, at the United Nations, in Washington, London, or Ankara—and may well be again.

Election day was about solidifying power at home, for the KDP in the KRG—the Kurdish Regional Government, the parliament of Iraqi Kurdistan—and for the united Kurdish ticket in the Iraqi Parliament. Before the arrival of Massoud and Nechirvan at the small one-room school in Salahaddin, Barzani family members and local operatives had been working hard at getting out the vote. When I arrived with Peter Galbraith and his son, peshmerga were lined up patiently awaiting their turn. The arrival of Massoud and Nechirvan caused a great stir: the cheering crowd of would-be voters divided to allow the two to make their way into the small classroom. Photographers, Kurdish and foreign, jostled for position. The excitement about the election was a clear indication that the Kurdish leadership had decided to hitch its future, at least for the time being, to the sweeping and ambitious political plans of America and the coalition partners. Though the election was the "liberators'" priority, it was for the Kurds a step toward their own future, an act of citizenship that excluded the foreigners, a move toward a more secure, less precarious form of self-determination.

An elderly woman was exiting the voting booths just before the Barzanis' arrival. She was all in black, with head covered and her abaya draped over her wheelchair, the finger the poll keepers had stained purple to indicate that she had voted standing out against her wintry-gray skin. A crew of peshmerga carried her down the building's steps just as they had carried her up. The purposeful serenity of her face never failed, not when the six armed men bearing her tipped her chair so that she almost fell out of it, and not when photographers surrounded her to capture the shot of fighters aiding an elderly woman on the first election day in the new Iraq. Looking at her, it was impossible to guess what she was feeling and whether she cared that she was being thrust into a spectacle. She had, I discovered, voted early and more than once. She would have most likely cast a vote for the united Kurdish list in the Iraqi Parliament and for the KDP in the KRG. But there was also a second vote at Kurdish polling centers that day. If the old woman went along with more than 90 percent of the population in Iraqi Kurdistan, she would have voted yes in an unofficial referendum on Kurdish independence.

"Our armies do not come into your cities and land as conquerors or enemies, but as liberators," the British major general Sir Stanley Maude comforted Baghdadis as his army entered the former capital of the caliphate in 1917. Conquerors or liberators, the undermanned invading army, followed by the well-schooled but at times ignorant colonial bureaucracy, soon faced a violent revolt. The basic parallels between the administration of the British Mandate of the 1920s, which followed the "liberation" by Maude's forces, and the American-led liberation and occupation of today are remarkable and well documented. Among the differences between the two ambitious acts of nation building, however, a couple of basic ones stand out: the British installed a monarch, whereas the Americans established a republic; furthermore, though the British may have failed to unite Iraq as a country, they did accomplish the clear delineation of its borders, within which a country could coalesce. For all the admirable intentions implied in trying to institute a liberal democracy, the effect of the American effort has been a loosening of ties and an unleashing of violence among Iraq's various ethnic and sectarian groups, and even less national cohesion than in colonial days. Ninety years after General Maude entered Baghdad, the Kurds of Iraq have yet to gain independence, but circumstances have allowed them at last to exploit autonomy to the point of being de facto independent, virtually a separate state.[1] In 2005, the Kurdish Regional Government in Arbil commissioned a series of television advertisements to promote foreign investment in the Kurdistan region. The ads were subsequently released on a DVD as *The Other Iraq*. Accompanying the three thirty-second spots was another film, *Who Are the Kurds?* The video portrays Iraqi Kurdistan as tolerant, secular, and diverse, before concluding: "This is how Kurdistan has always been, long before the country of Iraq ever existed."[2] And long after Iraq has ceased to exist?

This is not to say that the Kurds in Iraq have been entirely or unremittingly restive. The relationship between the Kurds and Baghdad has seen a range of vicissitudes. When the League of Nations gave Great Britain the mandate in 1920, three years after the fall of Ottoman-controlled Baghdad, the Treaty of Sèvres promised the Kurds an autonomous homeland. Amid new Turkish pressure, however, the promise was soon nullified and the British found themselves rather unexpectedly governing a diverse and undefined land. The British had envisioned annexing only Basra, into which they had marched in 1914 at the start of the war and where they find themselves again today, owing to that acquaintance. It was in the course of this confusing flux, and with the approval of the League of Nations, that southern Kurdistan—much of it located in the old Ottoman *vilayet* of Mosul—was included in the formation of the state of Iraq.

There is no denying that some Kurdish resistance to the central government in Baghdad, no matter who was in charge, has existed almost from those earliest days, with cultural issues such as language and education often producing sparks of grievance. Kurdish groups rebelled against the British in 1919, in an uprising led by Sheikh Mahmud Barzinji, and again in 1922. In 1931, a year before Iraq entered the League of Nations, a third revolt was suppressed only with the help of the RAF. Kurdish unrest was quelled, for a time anyway.[3]

Low-intensity conflict, with spikes of violence, continued throughout the twentieth century. The early 1960s and early 1970s saw sustained periods of armed resistance to Baghdad's control. And so the decisive uprising of 1991, which set Kurdistan on the path toward partial autonomy following the first Gulf War, may have arisen organically and spontaneously in cities like Raniyya and Kirkuk, but it drew upon this legacy of insurrectionary spirit.

The persistence of violence and revolt, however, does not negate the fact of a parallel tradition of Kurds playing a crucial role both in Baghdad and in Iraqi institutions such as the army. Indeed, Kurds were, in the early 1930s, overrepresented in high-ranking government posts: they occupied 22 percent of these offices though they made up only 17 percent of the population. (Shiites, on the other hand, were underrepresented by some thirty percentage points.)[4] Nor did the Kurds abstain from the persecution of minorities. In 1933, Kurdish tribesmen joined Bakr Sidqi in the massacre of the Assyrians to help solidify army power and prestige in the new state.[5] Assimilation of a sort continued as the KDP chose to hold its founding congress in Baghdad in August 1946.[6] By 1958 Kurds had penetrated the upper reaches of Iraqi government: Nuri Sa'id, who served as Iraqi prime minister numerous times, both during the mandate and after, during independence, had two Kurdish ministers. And Ahmad Mukhtar Baban, who followed Sa'id as prime minister—the last before the fall of the monarchy—was the first Kurd to become premier, albeit very briefly.

Kurdish influence in Baghdad has been on the decline more or less since the Baathist takeover of Iraq in the mid-1960s. Beginning in the mid-1970s, the nationalistic KDP Kurds in Baghdad were increasingly replaced by ones who were, according to one historian, "ready to collaborate."[7] Furthermore, what positions Kurds did receive declined steadily in importance. Of the five ministerial posts held by Kurds in 1982, four were without portfolio.

One more dimension of the relationship between the Kurds and the Iraqi government should be briefly mentioned: diplomacy, the gray area between conflict and politics. Facing steady violence in the north, despite the presence of Kurdish politicians in central Iraq, the government in Baghdad was often forced to deal with the internal Kurdish problem on the international stage. Leaders like Sheikh Mahmud Barzinji and Mullah Mustafa Barzani were both exiled to Iran, but were invited back in efforts to prevent further unrest and promote stability. Neither effort—those of the central government for control or of the nationalists for independence—would ever succeed so long as Baghdad thwarted Kurdish nationalist aspirations and so long as foreign powers, particularly Iran and the United States, continued to use the Kurds as a lever against the Iraqi government. During the uprising of 1974, the Iranian government, with the help of a young man named Ahmed Chalabi, provided Mullah Mustafa with additional fighting forces as well as light and long-range field guns, only to withdraw financial and military support under the March 1975 Algiers Agreement. The agreement settled for a time the Iran-Iraq tensions; the Iranians suspended aid to the Kurds in exchange for, most importantly, a more favorable demarcation of the Shatt al Arab river border (an arrangement Saddam repudiated when he invaded Iran in 1980). In the repression that followed in 1977 and 1978, some six hundred Kurdish villages were burned. The United States, which had been backing Kurdish forces, also began to slowly decrease support. It is difficult to separate any of the regional politics from the Cold War, and until Soviet relations with Iraq cooled following the Soviet invasion of Afghanistan and the Iraqi invasion of Iran a year later, the Kurds figured in American containment of the USSR's Baathist ally. In short, Kurdish leaders have had to navigate not simply the politics of Baghdad, but also those of Washington, Moscow, and Ankara.

Two days after the election we traveled into PUK territory to spend a few days in Suleymania. Kirkuk had voted for a separate Kurdish government when King Faisal was installed in 1921; Suleymania had simply refused to vote. Nearly eighty-three years later, however, at the home of Jalal Talabani, the talk was of nothing but elections and the hard road of history leading to them.

Whereas the Kurdish capital of Arbil is commonly described as Middle Eastern in feel, Suley, as Westerners often refer to it, is more Mediterranean. Walls of the city's crowded thoroughfares are painted with idyllic images of nature. On the grounds of a former army barracks belonging to Saddam, the PUK leadership has built a place for the locals to meet, walk, and entertain themselves. At the site of mass graves unearthed after the Baathists were deposed, the city's officials had built a Freedom Park, with a roller rink and flower-lined walkways. Dated Western pop music could be heard booming throughout the space. On the park's edge, a city bus passed by with a faded picture of Britney Spears from the late 1990s in the window.

Mum (Uncle) Jalal, as he is known in Iraqi Kurdistan, is a lively and charismatic figure. Though not particularly tall, he seems to weigh nearly three hundred pounds; he moves with the slow deliberateness of Marlon Brando in *The Freshman*. In his compound before dinner, Talabani was seated in the center of a sofa, on his right Kosrat Rasul and on his left Dr. Barham Salih. Rasul is a former PUK prime minster and a notorious pesh-merga, a household name in Kurdistan, famous in some homes as a patriot, infamous in others as a merciless soldier. He wore his Western suit awkwardly, his wandering eye befitting his legend: a soldier at heart, always scanning the room, unable to adapt to the relaxed safety of compounds and spacious offices. Salih, in contrast, was the picture of European elegance, gently unbuttoning the brass buttons of his blazer and folding one leg of his neatly pleated trousers over the other. He smoked Cohibas and spoke English with the hint of a British public school accent. As deputy to the interim prime minister, Ayad Allawi, he survived a dramatic attempt on his life in 2004 and had appeared more recently in the pages of the *Financial Times* and on cable news in the U.S.

Soon conversation turned to the subject of ministerial posts in the new Iraqi government. The Kurds, having apparently done very well in the national election, expected to fill ministerial seats in Baghdad. But even the extended speculation about likely contenders and desired positions always returned some-how to the subject of Kurdish autonomy and independence. This was the bloc politics of Iraq and the habit of these politi-cians was to think first of Kurdistan and then of Iraq. In this con-versation, however, with plenty of red wine and lamb on the table, Talabani was relatively expansive, allowing that northern Iraq's fate was increasingly shared with that of other regions. He fumed about the previous year's terrorist attacks in Arbil, noting that they were plotted in Mosul. Security for one part of the country, he suggested, required stability in all parts. The man who would soon be the first democratically elected president of Iraq declared emphatically, in more statesmanly than partisan terms, as his fist pounded his knee not far from his belly, "If we are to be in this Iraq, we must crush them"—referring to the insurgents.

As toasting abated and dinner reached its conclusion, the interim minister of water resources, Dr. Abdul Latif Rashid, spoke in understated platitudes. "These have been challenging and interesting times," he said. He had been instrumental in attempting to revive the wetlands of southern Iraq for the Marsh Arabs (the ecosystem that had sustained them for thousands of years had been systematically destroyed by Saddam), and he spoke dismissively of the constant rocket attacks on his office. Then he said, about Saddam's horrors, "It just means so much more if we remember those times."

On February 15, 1991, just prior to the American invasion that would expel Saddam and the Iraqi army from Kuwait, President George H. W. Bush encouraged the Iraqi military and the Iraqi people to "take matters into their own hands." While the statement might be open to some interpretation, the subsequent Kurdish uprisings were quite definitive. On March 5, 1991, the residents of the Kurdish city of Raniyya took up arms against Saddam's rule. Suleymania and Dohuk eventually joined in and the resource-rich city of Kirkuk soon fell under peshmerga control, as did much of the rest of Iraqi Kurdistan. At one point, the Shia uprising in the south, which also began in March, and the Kurdish in the north left Saddam with control of only four of the country's eighteen provinces. It was, however, a short-lived victory; when the U.S. government forces declined to topple Saddam, he turned his attention northward and heavy artillery and helicopter gunships advanced steadily to reclaim lost territory. Over one million refugees fled his army. From the Kurdish perspective, it was yet another abandonment by the West. Talabani and Barzani appealed to Bush directly, hoping to impress a moral obligation for action upon the U.S. president: "You personally called upon the Iraqi people to rise up against Saddam Hussein's brutal dictatorship." Support did not immediately arrive and, again, as they had many times before, the Iraqi Kurds had rebelled, only to find their situation unimproved—in fact, for the moment, it had dramatically worsened.[8]

The uprising that had started so spectacularly ended disastrously. Eventually, coalition troops were forced to move into Dohuk and create a safe zone in northern Iraqi Kurdistan to relieve the developing refugee crisis. The humanitarian disaster had forced the foreign powers to snatch a small but substantial victory for the Kurds from what could have been a resounding defeat.

Despite successful parliamentary elections, the first six years of autonomy were incredibly troubled ones. In 1994, around 1,000 soldiers (and perhaps more than 3,000) died in KDP-PUK infighting and more than 70,000 people were displaced.[9] Fighting began again in 1996 as PUK forces claimed Arbil only to lose it and also Suleymania to the KDP, which had been reinforced by 30,000 Iraqi troops. Making a bargain with the devil, the KDP had sought the perennial oppressor's help against their Kurdish brethren. Such internal division had led to the deaths of thousands of Kurds and to hardened pessimism on the street. It was also during this time that Islamist groups began to thrive in the normally secular autonomous region.[10]

The recourse to Baathist help was particularly heinous in light of the tyrant's most recent atrocities. On March 15, 1988, while the Kurds were still under his government, Saddam had attacked the town of Halabja with chemical shells, killing five thousand civilians. It was the peak of his *Anfal* campaign—a term taken from the Koran, meaning spoils of war—which drove hundreds of thousands of Kurds from their villages and left a profound effect upon the Kurdish psyche. Thereafter the Kurds could never imagine themselves out of the tyrant's reach. A year before the 1991 uprising, Izzat Ibrahim al-Duri, one of Saddam's deputies, warned upon a visit to Suleymania: "If you have forgotten Halabja, I would like to remind you that we are ready to repeat the operation."[11] Old memories die hard. With Saddam's troops located just to the south, insecurity remained even after autonomy. At the beginning of the war in March 2003, Arbil was deserted by many who feared another of Saddam's gas attacks.

The fledgling autonomous region was also hampered, oddly enough, by the unintended consequence of the UN sanctions, which began just as the Kurds set about convening their first parliament in 1992. Saddam cut Iraqi Kurdistan off from the rest of the country; the UN cut it off from the rest of the world. Much of the region went without electricity in the first half of the 1990s as the energy created there was funneled through Baghdad. The equipment needed to divert the power to Kurdistan was banned by the UN sanctions. Similarly, the matériel needed to uncap oil wells sealed by Saddam's troops was not allowed into the country. A UN survey in 2000 found the employment situation in Iraqi Kurdistan to be similar to that in the rest of Iraq. Between 5 and 10 percent of the population was jobless, and nearly 30 percent of the adult population, true to the *rentier*-state/bureaucracy model used by the Baathists, was employed in "government services."[12]

Despite these similarities to the Baathist example, and many failings that were entirely their own, Kurdish regional governments did demonstrate some capacity to deliver basic services.

Child mortality rates were lower than in the rest of Iraq. Two universities were established in the twelve years of autonomy, and the number of schools at all levels tripled. The number of hospitals grew faster than at any time in the region's history. Indeed, the *Report on the Transition to Democracy in Iraq,* produced in December 2002 by the controversial opposition group the Iraqi National Congress, acknowledged the stable and reasonably successful nature of the Kurdish autonomous region. With regards to maintaining the integrity of the state and the government after the fall of the Baathist regime, the document noted: "Within Iraq, only Iraqi-Kurdistan, with its two regional governments in Erbil and Suleimaniya, is equipped to respond to the needs of the situation."[13] It later added: "The Iraq body politic outside of the Kurdish regions will find itself the day after the fall of the regime formless and atomized."[14] Iraqi opposition groups expected—and would eventually convince their American patrons to expect—a vacuum, one that they hoped to fill with ideas and skills that had been developed in, among other places, Kurdistan. "The driving force behind the injection of this new idea, federalism," the document's authors noted, "has been the Kurdish experience in northern Iraq." After decades of acrimonious relations with Baghdad, the Kurds had become part of the talent base that would, in this vision, rebuild Iraq. The Kurdish region during autonomy was being held as an experimental prototype of what the rest of Iraq might look like—and overcoming the challenges of diversions and diversity were very much a part of that.

The political schism between the KDP and the PUK is based upon a myriad factors: tribal loyalties, patronage, delivery of services, a history of violence. It is not, however, the only division within Kurdish society. So many accounts portray the Kurds as a homogeneous group within the realm of Iraqi politics that the heterogeneity of northern Iraq is often forgotten. There are Christians—both Assyrians and Chaldeans—as well as Yazidis, who number in the tens of thousands and whose religion, often confused for devil worship, combines Zoroastrianism, Islam, and Christianity. In some places the minority representation is high. The population of Shaqlawa, a town ninety minutes from Arbil, is roughly 50 percent Christian. Its school (used on election day as a polling center) is located on the top of a hill off the village's main road. On election day in January 2005, no cars were allowed to park near the hill's bottom and peshmerga maintained a security presence on the school's roof. At the building's entrance and at the beginning and end of every hallway one passed through, soldiers were stationed, screening voters for firearms and explosives. The desks that once filled classrooms were scattered about the building, spilling out into play yards. Old men in baggy traditional Kurdish trousers squeezed themselves into the desk seats. Young men wearing jeans and carrying cell phones lounged atop desks they had sat behind just a few years ago. All stayed watchful of the comings and goings of voters and took special interest in their American visitors. It was an odd mix of block party and political rally and the supervised exercise hour of a prison.

Kurds are, for the most part, much more liberal regarding the rights of women than are the Arab Sunni and Shia of Iraq. In Voting Room #2, the registrar, the official in charge of assistance, and the ballot taker were all women. While a fair number of husbands escorted their wives step-by-step through the process, many women entered and exited without any male assistance. Younger women came in chatty groups by themselves.

Soon, amid the election excitement and the visit of Dr. Mohammed Ihsan (then the KRG's minister of human rights), a dispute broke out. Women, a representative of the Kurdistan

Islamic Union claimed, probably with some accuracy, were being pressured in their votes. Dr. Ihsan should know, the representative felt, that the Islamic party was being unfairly treated. The representative caused such a fuss that the voting room had to be shut down, as the orderly assembly gave way to a maelstrom of yelling between Islamists and other voters. A politician of skill as well as one of physical stature, Dr. Ihsan had left the Kurdistan region for a number of years to pursue a Ph.D. at the London School of Economics. He tried in his dignified way to calm the room but the Kurdistan Islamic Union representative continued his litany of complaint just inches from his chin.

Representatives from the KDP, the Islamic Union representative charged, were telling people how to vote. When confused voters had questions, he continued, especially the women, officials from the Kurdish parties were joining them in the booths. As his charges continued, the room grew louder, and the responses from the room's burgeoning number of self-declared "election experts" grew more heated.

The complaint was a valid one, Dr. Ihsan responded circumspectly, attempting to restore order, although voters had the right to ask for help. Armed with this ruling from a minister and their own evaluation of the election procedures, the majority of the group took to berating the protester. Feeling put-upon, by both officialdom and those around him, the representative responded in kind. Moving from defense to offense, he escalated his accusation from voting irregularities to widespread fraud.

Having retreated to a corner of the classroom to observe the mounting chaos, I was approached by a national election official who began to speak in broken English. After we exchanged names, he proudly displayed the lanyard from which his election badge hung. Believing that he was drawing attention to the Nokia logos imprinted on it every few inches, I complimented him on his gear. I mistakenly came to think of this as the Nokia theory of international friendship—if I and this fifty-something man from a hillside village in Iraqi Kurdistan had nothing else in common, we could always chat pleasantly about the relative merits of mobile phone manufacturers. But my mention of Nokia confused him. What had been a look of excitement and pride turned to a stare of insult and misunderstanding. I tried again, pointing to the Nokia logo and saying, "Good phones," showing him mine.

Now certain that I had missed the point, he grabbed the red lanyard again, this time explicitly indicating its color rather than the brand name: "Red. I am a Communist. You see it's red. Me Communist. Are you Communist?"

Not a question one hears every day. Despite my surprise, my reply was almost reflexive: "No. No, I am not a Communist."

Looking slightly hurt, he tried again: "You are not a Communist?" I shook my head more decisively: no, I am not. Stopping for a moment to think, he looked away until another way occurred to him. As if it were the most logical follow-up he said: "Chicago. Chicago is a nice city."

"It's a great city," I replied, smiling.

"I have friend in Chicago, some day I go," he continued, "I'm a Christian. Are you a Christian?"

I nodded yes and my Chicago-loving Christian Communist friend and I shook hands and parted ways. Just a couple of seconds later, the dispute between the Islamists, the KDP faithful, and the election officials was resolved. For a brief moment, at least, Dr. Ihsan had led them to see shared interests, easing the tension just as my friend and I had dispelled the awkwardness between us with the discovery of common faith and a common notion of urban excellence. The minister of human rights did it on a grander scale of about thirty, by reminding them that this was an election for Kurdistan and for Iraq, obliging them for a day either to stand together or to stand apart amicably. He hadn't the power to validate or invalidate the voting but he did have the intelligence and character to point out to people what they ought to respect in one another—an admirable end to an imperfect day.

In great numbers in Basra and Baghdad, in small numbers in Falluja and Mosul, Iraqis braved the threat of violence to turn out and vote. In the Kurdistan region, security forces prevailed and there was no violence. In the capital and elsewhere, some voters were not as fortunate. At least thirty-four Iraqis died in shootings and bombings. It was democracy the hard way. The results would be nearly two weeks in coming, but to nobody's great surprise, most voted their identity. Reducing the voting to results or participation to numbers, however, does injustice to the countless small acts of reconciliation, mediation, compromise, protection, determination, and encouragement that occurred on this day. Most of these small acts would quickly fade out of memory as the government failed to convene and the violence only escalated. The efforts of people like Mohammed Ihsan to smooth over potentially violent disagreements cleared the way for young women and their crippled elderly grandmothers to vote. And, lest it be totally forgotten, many did exactly that.

5. English I: Travel, Globalization, and Hollywood

BY *the second week of classes, I had been assigned two guards. Though neither of them spoke much English, they both spent most nights watching undubbed American movies on satellite television. After class sometimes, I would go over to the house of Azad, the elder guard, and watch television for a few hours. His wife would shuffle in and out with tea, while his young daughter crawled around on the floor. A Kalashnikov rested in the corner; his pistol sat next to it. Azad, who had been a butcher before he went into the security business, would watch music videos before the movies started and look over at me in confusion when a guitarist burned his instrument or Beyoncé swam in a gigantic champagne glass. Azad had few points of reference for distinguishing the real from the staged in the sometimes absurd world of music videos. He made $250 a month. Some Americans spend that on a pair of jeans with holes in them. What's to stop them from bathing in champagne?*

Sarhang, the younger of the two guards at twenty-five, learned English at an astonishing rate. Near the beginning of the term, he had watched Braveheart, *pointedly using the word "freedom" the next day. Some weeks before I was to leave, the movie station ran* The Patriot, *another Mel Gibson film. On the way to class on a Saturday, Sarhang asked me if I knew the movie. He was curious to know more about American history, he said, and let me know how very exciting it was that William*

Wallace had fought the English in Scotland and then traveled to America to fight them again.

Three miles from the college at which I was teaching American history, past a makeshift soccer field in a taxi parking lot and a brand-new Toyota dealership, was Salahaddin University's new Social and Cultural Center. It is an eclectic building, a rough draft of Richard Rogers and Renzo Piano's Pompidou Centre merged with Miami art deco. Amid the city's faded concrete, bricks, and dust, it stands out for both its ambition and its eccentricity. Beginning with the spring term of my arrival, the building housed Salahaddin's new Language Center. Nearly a year after Saddam's fall, Dr. Mohammed Sadik replaced the former Baathist who had run the university. Having received his Ph.D. in Edinburgh and raised his children in the United Kingdom, the new president had an eye toward the West; he arranged classes so his professors and teachers could improve their English and French. The inaugural semester began with over sixty students enrolled for English and none for French.

Some of the university's staff were required to attend the class, while nearly twenty deans, professors, and students enrolled electively. The rest of the group was a mix of government officials, liaisons with nongovernmental organizations (NGOs), and entrepreneurial businessmen. General Diler came from the police department. A sort of modern Middle Eastern Sherlock-Holmes-meets-Oscar-Wilde, he wore a trenchcoat over his dapper suits, and was never without a flower in his lapel. Diler was chief of forensics studies for the Kurdistan region and taught fingerprinting and ballistics at the heavily guarded police academy down the street. He had held a high-ranking position in the capital until 1990, but fled from Saddam after the first Gulf War and the Kurdish uprising.

Jihad, a skinny man in his mid-forties, had worked as director of one of the region's leading land-mine-education NGOs. Three weeks into the course, he gave me a set of prayer beads and showed me how they could be used not just for praying, but also for swinging, "while you dance," he added with a smile. Walking with a discernible limp, he entered rooms quietly, as if always preoccupied. There was the dancing side to him as well, however, and conversation rarely failed to draw him out of quiet reflection into an eager, though always respectful, agitation.

With an approachable demeanor that belied his piercing eyes, Mahir was the class's most notable student. His wavy black hair, handsome face, and modest but attractive suits were familiar to all. He was one of Kurdistan's pop stars, featured on television and on the cover of CDs at the bazaar. Immediately recognizable, he was greeted with handshakes and nods and other affectionate gestures.

There was also a software writer and an emergency room doctor. There were three brothers, all engineers, all balding and overweight, with deep laughs and broad smiles. There were two young, religiously conservative and excitable Mohammeds and one elder Mohammed, more liberal and subdued, who lectured at the College of Sharia, or Islamic law. There were deans with the air of Oxford dons, young business owners with the confidence of would-be Donald Trumps, and secretaries, retirees-to-be, and interlopers who had heard about the class at the bazaar. They were, with the exception of a few students, of a different generation from those I was teaching history. They had seen and endured more violence. They had rebelled and compromised. Stability, rather than opportunity, seemed to be their chief concern.

In addition to me, there were three other teachers, all of whom had grown up in the West but had family in greater Kurdistan. The role of former Iraqi exiles in encouraging the

U.S. invasion and in helping to lead their country after they returned home has been widely documented. Ahmed Chalabi developed a network of relationships in the 1990s that allowed him to lobby American officials and publicize the desire within Iraq to see Saddam go. Ayad Allawi, who had worked with the CIA and lived in London, returned to Baghdad and became the unelected interim prime minister. In the Kurdistan region, men like Dr. Mohammed, the president of the university, had returned to play a role in the new direction of their country. But also in the north were many less heralded, ordinary Kurds who had come to work in a country in which they had never lived. My three fellow teachers, Mahtab, Bayan, and Djene, were three of them—children of Kurds in either Europe or North America, who had never set foot in Iraq until 2003. Mahtab was a stunningly attractive young woman who was often dressed like she was heading to the beach in L.A. rather than teaching in Arbil. An Iranian Kurd, she epitomized nineteenth-century European ideals of Oriental beauty. Djene and Bayan were a couple, but rather than deal with the controversy, gossip, and scorn that inevitably attended a relationship without a ring, they simply introduced themselves as husband and wife. Bayan was the daughter of Iranian Kurds who had fled to London after the Islamic Revolution in 1979. Djene, his father Kurdish and his mother Welsh, had taken a year off between London's School of Oriental Studies and the London School of Economics to return to his father's country and teach. None of the three would describe their decisions to come to Arbil as idealistic or even admirable. They were paid poorly and suffered with the disorganized bureaucracy, but they considered it natural that they should learn the language of their parents, see part of their ancestral homeland, and hopefully contribute to its future.

The four of us spent the first day administering an exam to sort the class by skill level. A handful of deans and one government official sensed in this exam a challenge to the hierarchy of the status quo, one that threatened to place them below students and secretaries, and they responded preemptively by insisting on lengthy interviews or by offering dragged-out answers to brief written questions. I ended each interview with the simple question, "Why do you want to study English?"

"It is the language of science," answered a professor of physics.

A dean replied that he needed to improve his English to communicate better with colleagues in America using the Internet.

"It is the language of business," offered an administrative worker.

Many hoped one day to visit America or England.

One of the last students we interviewed spoke very little English, struggled to find an answer, and then offered a simple response: "It is the language of the world."

Alexis de Tocqueville, a Frenchman who wrote about America in the nineteenth century, noted, "The bond of language is perhaps the strongest and most durable that exists among men." It was no longer one shared across Iraq. Many of the younger students in the group knew little Arabic and others refused to use it at all. Arabic may have been the predominant language of Iraq, but Kurdish was the language of autonomy in the north—a linguistic split that had plagued Iraqi politics, particularly in regard to education, since the nation's formation. They had no reservations, however, about developing their English. They were friends of the West and America in particular and saw in the new order an opportunity for improvement. They came from a range of backgrounds and generations, the oldest and youngest students some forty years apart in age. The first day's hints of frustration at the lack of attention to social hierarchy had become a significant problem by the second. Insulted by the notion of studying with people of lesser position, a number of deans said the classes should not go forward.

Complaints filtered though the active university rumor mill. While respect for position and title is certainly part of Kurdish and Iraqi culture, this was something else: an exaggerated and irrational claim of status and importance; the legacy of privilege, order, and dependency bred by a dictatorship that ran on patronage as well as violence.

Dr. Khalid was one of these reluctant professors. He was missing a front tooth, had short graying hair thinning in the front, and always seemed to get the pant legs of his suit caught in his shoes. Like Diler, he often wore a flower in his lapel, but since the flower was always nearer to rotting rather than to blooming, it held little charm. Rumor had it that in the 1980s, he had written as his dissertation in Baghdad a favorable account of Saddam Hussein's human rights record—a subject he still taught at the university, though presumably with less favorable discussion of Saddam. He had toed the line, played by the rules that had become engrained within him—but now they had changed. And to his credit, he too was changing, but not without making his displeasure heard.

De Tocqueville pointed out the danger posed to democracy and progress by the bureaucratic and hierarchical habits of authoritarianism:

> If a democratic republic like the one in the United States were ever to be established in a country where autocratic rule had already introduced administrative centralization, and where both custom and law had absorbed its influence, that country would come to know a despotism more intolerable than any that has ever existed in Europe's absolute monarchies.[1]

Although the despotism anticipated by the passage may not have set in by 2005, it was already clear that extirpating the legacy of autocracy would require more than toppling the autocrat. Old institutions and habits were certainly complicating the business of establishing new ones in Iraq.

According to the historian and political scientist Isam al-Khafaji, who worked with American officials in Baghdad in 2003 before resigning in protest over the administrative approach of the occupation's governing body, the Coalition Provisional Authority (CPA), Saddam's regime accounted for over 20 percent of the civilian employment, meaning that 40 percent of Iraqi households directly depended upon government money. In *Inventing Iraq,* the historian Toby Dodge estimates that between 1958 and 1977, the number of Iraqis in nonmilitary government service expanded from 20,000 to 580,000. Writing of Kut, a city of 350,000 in the Wasit province in the Shiite-dominated south of Iraq, Mark Etherington, the British CPA chief there in 2004, observed, "While they were content to discuss the issues of the day, they were loath to take decisions. This resulted from a kind of generational deformity: Saddam Hussein's security system had made such discussion, let alone action, unthinkable." Whether it was professors refusing to study alongside their secretaries or security officials refusing to allow the public access to a city park—believing it still to be, as it had been in the past, the special domain of public officials—the learned habits of Saddam's dictatorship remained embedded in everyday life.[2]

Travel

The Language Center was staffed by two university officials, one a kindly and dedicated Ph.D. who did not often interfere with lessons and another who made a habit of interrupting class to take attendance. At the beginning of the term, the office had two desks, no computers, and a collection of boxed materials sent by USAID to encourage the study of English. They had lain there for months, unopened, and largely would remain so: the cartoon drawings and grammar exercises were deemed unsuitable to keeping the attention of adults. If, as Woody Allen quipped, showing up counts for 80 percent in life, it counted 100 percent in determining the course material for this first term.

As I had just arrived from New York, Mahtab from Canada, Bayan from London, and Djene from the north of England, travel became the first week's theme. Having limited Kurdish and no Arabic, I was assigned to teach conversation and reading comprehension to the advanced group, who had intermediate English skills. We stumbled through the confusing discrepancies of British and American English. Round-trip or return? Single or one-way? Hire or rent? As in my history class, I was the first American most students in the class had met and spoken with; mine was the first American accent they had heard in person. All of their previous instructors had been speakers of English as a second language with British accents acquired through either a British education or the BBC World Service. The sudden realization that English was no more monolithic than Kurdish, for example, was bewildering. "Two countries divided by a common language," as Shaw described the Anglo-American relationship. Confusing and unnecessarily complicated was how my students saw it. Wasn't it enough that they were dedicating themselves to learning English? Must they now learn not one language but two?

"Which is the most popular English?" an aging professor of physics asked.

"Well," Dr. Khalid moaned, turning his shoulders away from the front of the room in a stubborn sulk, "how am I ever going to know to say 'coach' or 'bus'?"

As if the Atlantic divide were not enough, our first reading comprehension exercise came from a rather anachronistic section of *Lonely Planet: England* that Djene downloaded from the

World Wide Web. It started: "While the Family may have taken a right Royal battering, many of the other august institutions at the cornerstone of British life have muddled their way through with a stiff upper lip and a strong sense of protocol." The passage only got better as it turned to recreation:

> For the sporty, the traditional Oxford/Cambridge University Boat Race is held in London on the River Thames in late March/early April; the famous but grueling Grand National steeplechase takes place at Aintree, Liverpool . . . The Lawn Tennis Championships, complete with strawberries and cream, and tantrums by major players, take place at Wimbledon in late June; in the same month the champagne-quaffing set head for the Henley Royal Regatta at Henley-on-Thames; and the Cowes Yachting pushes off on the Isle of Wight in late July/early August.

In sparking discussion of travel, anachronistic and incongruous references were far from our biggest challenge. "Tell me about planning a trip to England," I suggested. Silence. Imagining the proposition too exotic, I tried somewhere closer to home. "How about a recent trip to Istanbul?" Nothing. There was disagreement about when the train from Arbil to Baghdad had operated; but none had ever been on it. There was, rumor had it, a train from Mosul to Damascus, but no one could state with certainty when, if ever, the train had run or how long the trip had taken. Among the powerful and privileged students in the class, only one had been to Damascus, a handful to Tehran, and a couple more to Istanbul. One had been to London, two to the Soviet Union, none to the United States.

During the period of autonomy and regional conflict in the 1990s, Saddam loomed just fifty miles to the south, air travel was restricted by both infrastructure and financial limitations, and, for its own reasons, Turkey imposed daunting difficulties on car travel to the north. Going by way of Iran was an option in theory, but that made the trip prohibitively long and expensive.

Dictatorship goes beyond curtailing those freedoms that define liberal democracy. Josef Stalin, Saddam's role model and obsession, was said to have succeeded in "politicizing sleep"—no realm of individual experience was safe from his reach. An outsider, I had considered Saddam's monstrous violence, his egomania, and his cruel, luxurious camp appetites. One cannot, however, comprehend from the outside all the elements of a vision of "total control." Imagination—and the attendant faculties of empathy, sympathy, and compassion—I would tell my history students later in the term, is vital to understanding the past. What I had failed to imagine, and what my students continually labored to impress upon me, was the utterly disabling distraction of living day in, day out under or next to a murderous tyrant. Saddam did not arrive in northern Iraq when he invaded Kuwait, nor did he leave entirely when coalition forces entered in 2003. What had been for me a sporadic TV presence had been for my students an unending menace, from relatively innocuous reminders of his power to threats of more poison gas. One could never be sure how far he would go, and one had to plan accordingly. What would I have done if I had been called to fight in the war with Iran? If told to attack my own people? And how did one negotiate the subtler, less absolute dictates of the tyrant's will? I had not even considered these questions. Would I have dutifully closed my shop and suffered loss of income on a holiday in Saddam's honor? Would I have refused a friendly dinner invitation on account of having seen a small photo of Saddam on my would-be host's desk? I was trying to strike up conversation about a kind of freedom of movement that I took for granted, even as it related to making my way to Arbil. Many of my students had never left their home country, some did not have passports, and nearly half had never traveled more than three hundred miles from home. The same may be said of many Americans, of course, but these students had known little of choice or opportunity.

Two years after the fall of Baghdad, the travel situation had not improved much. International flights in and out of Arbil had yet to begin. There were rumors of impending service to Amman and Frankfurt, but these flights were very slow in coming, and when they did, in late 2005, the fares were beyond the means of a professor or dean, never mind a secretary or student. Train travel to Mosul, Baghdad, or Basra was a preposterous notion. Crowded trains traveling on scheduled routes at scheduled times would be catnip for insurgents. A country unable to keep crucial oil pipelines safe could hardly be expected to keep trains running. The trip out of northern Iraq by car was long, exhausting, and, at times, dangerous. The border at Zakho was frequently closed and Turkish intelligence officials often arbitrarily denied Kurds entry into the country. And so insecurity and geopolitics ensured that vacations were limited to the much-cherished Friday picnics in the hills. As for a trip to Greece or Lebanon, none in the class doubted that the freedom and means would come; it was just that the already long wait was going to be a little longer still.

If international travel seemed a barren subject, how about travel in Iraq? What is there to see in Mosul? A young woman, her head covered in *hejab,* and an owner of a concrete firm were the only two to respond. Neither offered anything verbal: separately but simultaneously each pantomimed a beheading with a sharp stroke of the right hand. Ominous as the gesture was, it drew giggles. "You can't go to Mosul," a student eventually said in a tone that implied an unspoken "silly!" Okay then, I continued, if not Mosul, how about Kirkuk? There were three Kirkukis in the class and they had spoken with pride about their city in our interviews. Again, giggles and chops to the neck.

Trefa, the young woman in *hejab* who had been first to draw her finger across her throat, was from Kirkuk. "We'll take you to Kirkuk. You can travel to Kirkuk with us. We'll go right after the term ends." There was again much laughter followed by another slashing motion or two. This was a deeply religious woman, who observed some of the stricter requirements in her clothing and had retreated from my extended hand when we first met. She had known personal loss at the hands of Saddam's murderers, when the police "disappeared" her eldest brother in the late 1980s. I answered her comment with a small, nervous smile. Her sense of humor was not as callous or indifferent as it may have seemed. Gallows humor, I came to see, was a natural defense in the face of frequent, random, and horrifying violence. When Trefa and I eventually did travel to Kirkuk together almost a year later, she leaned forward from the back seat, where custom bade her sit despite the increased risk of my being noticed in the front seat, and smiling at my head wrapped in a *kefiya* quipped, "Did you pray, Ian?" As the term went on, it had become clear that my students constantly worried about me: Did I have friends? Did I need some food? And most important, was I safe and protected? Their jokes, which continued throughout the term, were my students' awkward way of dealing with the last of those worries.

Knowing that, however, did not make the subject of decapitation for travel's sake more appealing. I tried a different tack, asking the class where they dreamed of going. When Iraqi or Kurdistan Air flies regularly, when Turkey eases up restrictions and the oil money starts to flow through society, what trip will you go on?

"I am not going on a trip. I haven't the money and I don't see what there is to think about," one replied rather gruffly, but others finally got into the swing of the exercise.

Dr. Kafea, a likable and earnest older woman, the dean of the nursing school, raised her hand and offered the practiced response diligently concatenating all the relevant vocabulary. "I will book a *round-trip* ticket, *connect* in Istanbul, claim my bags at *baggage claim*, ride a *bus* to town, and *check in* to my hotel, where I will have *room service*," she said. She never did tell us where she was going or why.

Another woman wanted to go to London and visit her nephew. Dr. Bokhari, a former peshmerga and professor of political science, who would become a member of the Iraqi Parliament in 2006, wanted to return to Ukraine, where he had studied in the 1970s.

Mohammed, a confident young man dressed in American designer knockoffs, wanted to visit his cousin in America. "He lives in Oshkosh," he said excitedly. "He is a head-cheese." He thought for a second and then corrected himself. "Not a head-cheese. He is a cheese-head, a cheese-head."

Globalization

Travel was a briefly entertaining but unyielding subject for conversation. The students were slowly adapting to my laid-back approach, to free-flowing discussion without regard to social station, but I was still looking for a topic that would engage both their interests and their experiences. As we returned for the second week of class, I heard that no one had spent the weekend beyond the outskirts of Arbil. Not until springtime would country picnickers be clogging roads into and out of the city. Winter typically led a few to the mountains, but most stayed inside with kerosene heat and television. Since venturing forth into the world was for the time being a remote prospect, I suggested we talk about the world that was coming to them. What I had in mind was not "hard power"—troops, tanks, and planes—but music, movies, and products, the stuff of "soft power," or globalization. "What is globalization?" has been asked in some form in just about every seminar room on every college campus in

America. Now, in a mix of English and Kurdish, my students . tried to answer it. They weren't struggling to translate answers they had prepared in international economics classes or recycled from textbooks. In fact, they seemed not to have been asked the question before, at least not in such simple terms. (It is, in fairness, a question that remains unanswered in most American classrooms.)

With a little encouragement, Mohammed with the cheesehead cousin gave it a try, "Globalization is communication. Like the cell phones and the Internet and the e-mail." As partial answers often do, this one unleashed a flood of clarification, expatiation, and contradiction: "I think business is the globalization. The Germans and the Turks in the hotels bring globalization." "It is the dollar. It is all about the dollar." "How about the televisions and the satellites?" "Science. More ideas about who we are and the body." "Yes. I think so. Also science. Machines and science come in globalization."

The class soon split into schools of thought, one arguing macroeconomics, another science and technology, and the third simple consumerism. Each camp was convinced that it had got to the heart of the matter with an ultimate definition of globalization. Could it be, I asked, that all three elements—as well as the movement of people, access to information, and an interdependent security situation—were part of the same worldwide phenomenon? The class was again united: of course not. As often happened throughout the term, the most difficult obstacle to fluent discussion was not contentious topics such as America or Islam, but a more general divergence of ways of seeing the world. I was an American and a teacher, and I was received respectfully by virtue of both designations. This is not to say, however, that the ideas and concerns I had absorbed during my education were guaranteed the same respect. These were not so much clashes as differences of perspective inevitably born of differences in experience. A soldier in his Humvee, behind body armor and a Mark-19, looks down blank-faced at an Iraqi man returning home from work; the Iraqi looks up equally without expression. Each sees the potential for violence and aggression in the other, though neither can quite see the other as the other sees himself. Sometimes their fears are justified. At other times, they are just two men from different worlds trying to make sense of a shared situation. At times, too, my students and I, having committed ourselves to communication and having no guns trained on us, could bridge the gulf of experience and see things in similar ways. At other times, however, the will or the means to do so were simply not available. Where I came from, globalization was an accepted concept for making sense of the world. My students did not see the need to agree.

In the previous ten years, the residents of Arbil had seen the arrival of satellite television and its three hundred and fifty channels. The selection of Western soft drinks and sugary cereals in the bazaar was ever expanding. American and British troops had swept through Iraq, some launched from Kurdish territories. Businesspeople from all over the world were now investing in their city, and South Korean troops, in an effort called Operation Green Angel, converged on outlying villages with soccer balls, bananas, and baked treats. Every day, students at the university accessed information from all over the world on South Korean computers via a network set up soon after the war's start by Arab, Kurdish, British, and American engineers. But my class did not see these events as part of a bigger shift in the way the world interacted.

They all agreed, though, that these changes had a common theme. Their own world was becoming more open. Before, under Saddam and even during autonomy, several explained, they had very little access to information and people. Few foreigners came to visit. Kurdish scientists and academics could not keep up with ideas in Turkey, let alone in America or Europe.

Now, the students said, echoing each other's excitement, they were in constant contact with people in the outside world. Now they were no longer isolated. Though nobody could agree on what globalization was exactly, most were prepared to allow it had something to do with these improvements.

If the purpose of any topic was to prompt conversation, this quick consensus posed a slight problem. I prodded: "Sure, there might be some good to these changes. But can't society maybe be too open? What if all the kebab restaurants in the bazaar are replaced by McDonald's? Could it harm Kurdish culture?" I looked out at a sea of dismissive smirks and blank stares.

Dr. Kafea, the dean of the nursing school, who wore modest long dresses and *hejab,* responded, "We lived under Saddam. There can't be too open. You see, before, all we could see on the television was that Israel was evil. That Israel was murdering people and was bad. Now we have many channels and we don't have to hear that anymore."

Influential thinkers in America like Joseph Nye, a former assistant secretary of state, and Fareed Zakaria, an editor at *Newsweek,* have both written about a phenomenon tied to the expansion of information sources. Amid the great flood of new choices, individuals are drawn to sites or channels that confirm what they already believe. Additionally, they become dependent upon what Nye calls "cue givers"—people who guide them to what they are looking for through the infinite sea of information and commentary now available.[3]

I challenged the class with this insight. Were not, I asked, all the options rendered somewhat irrelevant if you just watch the channels that tell you what you want to hear and read the Web sites that agree with you? The question drew the same response from just about every student: "Yes, maybe, but now we get to choose." By their lights I was quibbling about the consequences of too much choice.

Eventually the idea began to sink in that one could admire the general impulse of globalization and still be critical of various particulars. The religious conservatives, one woman and three men of devout sentiment, were first to embrace the notion that all the information and Western culture flooding into the Middle East might have its negative aspects.

"Sometimes the young people just watch the television and go to the Internet cafés or talk on their phones," suggested Trefa, the young Kirkuki woman, with disappointment, "and then skip prayer or do not go to the mosque." Similar views could be heard in the United States. The social effects of the current technological and commercial revolution, the ways entertainment culture drew attention away from activities that sustained traditional bonds: these concerns were not particular to the Muslim world. Here, however, the conflicts, like the technology, were relatively new, and the choices extreme.

"I think that, too, on the Internet and sometimes on the television our people can see things or watch things that aren't true with our religion," said Mohammed, an English teacher in his mid-twenties and one of the few men in the class who would not shake hands with women.

While some like Mohammed worried about the gradual effects of the media on religious piety, most of the students who had children expressed the more immediate concern shared by many parents in America: how to shield their children from "mature" subject matter, whether Janet Jackson's breast or the trendy cell phone video of a nude Lebanese pop star in the shower. There was notable consensus about how the problem should, or rather should not, be dealt with. No one in the class, from the most zealously religious to the atheistic Soviet-educated peshmerga clique led by Dr. Bokhari, advocated any form of oversight. Trefa did not recommend a new government-backed public dedication to the teachings of the Prophet. Dr. Bokhari, dismissive of religion and proud of his years in Ukraine, had no taste for letting the government monitor, never mind censor, Western-style sex and violence on his television.

"It is for our self to do it," said Mahir, the pop star who with his wife had a two-year-old son. "It is for the family to decide."

His opinion echoed through the class. "Each family can do it. It is the responsibility, with parents and grandparents," Dr. Bokhari added.

Another complex issue rendered relatively simple by the force of experience. While America was flirting with curtailing civil liberties for the sake of other goods, such as security and decency, here the recent attainment of rights after years of deprivation made compromise even for the sake of another good all but unthinkable. Government was not needed or wanted in the information sphere: it had been there long enough. Individual responsibility would have to suffice.

Thinking our discussion was nearing its end, I asked if there were any other elements we might add to our definition of globalization.

Without hesitation, and with his typical energy, Jihad, the mine-removal instructor, responded, "Also globalization is about the ability of one country to just invade others." Later in the term we would have extensive debates about America and the war in Iraq, but this was the first time they had grown comfortable enough with me to broach the subject. "It is about America and that America can just come into Iraq. And by itself. And Saddam and nobody can stop him."

Never once during the term did the students use any word but "liberation" when referring to the war in Iraq. "Occupation" and "invasion" were not yet in their vocabulary when it came to the American presence. But despite Jihad's professed admiration for America, indeed the entire class's approval of the "liberation," I could not help hearing in this comment a note of rebuke.

The sentiment was seconded by Bahadin, a young Iranian Kurd: "Yes, in some ways globalization is that America can do whatever it wants."

"For us this is good," Dr. Bokhari reminded the group.

"Yes, and hopefully they go to Iran too," Bahadin, whose father had been forced to leave Iran, replied. "I know this is good for us."

Jihad brought the conversation back from the specific to the general: "We all know this is good. But America, he can also just do what he wants."

Nobody had yet uttered the name of Osama bin Laden. What about Al Qaeda and September 11? I asked. Did the attacks on New York and Washington not show that in today's world individuals could wreak havoc on large numbers of people? Did not one man declare war on the world's largest power? The definitive effect of globalization, I suggested over the scoffing, was not the might of a single superpower but the inevitability of interdependence: America's security, like it or not, was tied to backwater provinces of Afghanistan.

This, the entire class agreed, perhaps not unreasonably, was nonsense. America was too big and too strong; no one man or small group could threaten it. The evidence said otherwise, I countered, now enjoying the rhythm of an energized backand-forth. Dedicated terrorists, airplane tickets, and box cutters were all it took to topple an international symbol of America's strength. Again the class dismissed the idea, but without quite addressing themselves either way to the events in lower Manhattan. America was simply too powerful in their eyes for the attacks to seem any more serious than a flea biting the rump of an ox. Yes, Al Qaeda and bin Laden (the class's near-unanimous view of whom would be revealed later in the term) had inflicted great damage on New York City, but that was hardly to say that individuals were in any position to decisively challenge the world's great powers.

Of course, this was not just about America. The inability to recognize the potential of "super-empowered individuals" (as *New York Times* columnist Thomas Friedman calls them) had more to do with Iraqi history. All had known at least two decades of Baathism. Some had spent years in the mountains as peshmerga fighting against Saddam. They were party to proud sacrifice and resistance that got limited results at a glacial pace. How could it be, then, that in this new world well-organized and -funded individuals could pose a threat to even more powerful states? The lesson of their history was that individuals slog and suffer, while great powers topple countries. While they never turned hostile or even defensive about the matter, they could not envision the individual as doing much more than endure and observe the course of things. Class ended just moments after the allotted two hours were up as Mohammed the English teacher reminded me that it was time for evening prayer.

Hollywood

Steven Spielberg? Blank stares. Tom Cruise? Anxious confusion. *Titanic?* It was still early in that day's four-hour class when everyone looked at me as if I was an idiot. Of course they knew *Titanic*, everybody knew *Titanic*. Fifty million Americans had seen the film, I was informed, and seemingly every Kurd. Just about any awkward silence—seated beside a stranger on a plane, on a chairlift with your girlfriend's dad, or in a barber's chair—can be banished with the question, "Seen any good movies lately?" It is safe—light, apolitical, and inoffensive. We had the week before discussed the direction of the world, and so something lighter was certainly in order. As it turned out, however, we could not talk about one of America's most popular exports without discussing the dictator America had overthrown.

It started innocently enough. We talked about genres. Some

of the older students remembered classics like *Gone with the Wind* and *Spartacus*.

One man loved "the cowboys."

Another said his favorites were the "mythology films."

"What is mythology films?" asked a fellow student.

Making use of new vocabulary, he replied: "The mythology genre. Like *Rambo*."

Every once in a while someone would just shout out the name of a film; by now I had sacrificed order to excitement over the material. *"Ghost,"* exclaimed a deep male voice.

"The Spider . . . *Spiderman,"* Trefa excitedly piped up.

Advancing through the vocabulary, we covered "concession stand," "box office," and "previews," none of which were familiar. I explained each as part of the experience of going to the movie theater. Somewhat surprised, General Diler, the dapper policeman, declared: "The theater is over. We just watch satellite. The theater is the old-fashion."

Traveling south from Baghdad, Mark Etherington, the CPA chief in Kut, passed by two very American images. "We drove past a water tower on which an American soldier had written 'I love you Diane Honey' within a giant red heart, and an open-air cinema with 'Now Showing: Operation Iraqi Freedom—starring U.S. Marine Corps' sprayed in black on its screen."4

In Dohuk, one of the northernmost cities of Iraqi Kurdistan, there was a single theater on the edge of the bazaar that sat empty most of the day. It showed, among other things, reruns of Pamela Anderson's *V.I.P.* Arbil, as it turned out, had perhaps as many as four theaters—and nobody in the class had been to any of them in the past thirty years. In fact, they did not even know what the theaters showed, if anything at all anymore.

"Westerns," said General Diler.

An idea the man who loved "cowboys" quickly corrected. "No," he blurted out defensively, "They show the kids' movies."

Mohammed the English teacher offered: "They show the movies of the sex."

Random outburst: "I love movies about engineering."

The class was as disparaging of Kurdish filmmaking as it was of the idea of going to the cinema. *Turtles Also Fly*, a film by an Iranian Kurd, had recently been submitted for Oscar consideration. A young man by the name of Mehmet Yasa had recently been described as "the Quentin Tarantino of Kurdish cinema." Yasa, however, like most other innovative Kurdish filmmakers, works out of Turkey, Diyarbakir in particular. Jano Rosebiani, another successful Iraqi Kurd filmmaker, had recently returned to Arbil after spending many years working abroad. A Kurdish film festival was up and running—in London. Most films by Kurds in Iraq, I was told, followed a rather routine plotline. "All the Kurdish films are romantic," suggested Dr. Kafea, after summarizing the plotline.

"And then they all end with tragedy," Jihad added, finishing the sentence for her.

The tale of Farhard and Sirih, the class explained, was an example: a Kurdish sculptor carves a monument to his love and then hurls himself off the mountain when his affection is spurned. The tale of unrequited love was as old as the epic of Gilgamesh claimed by some to be set in the nearby Zagros Mountains; it was all the students knew of Iraqi Kurdish film. There was no getting away from fate, the class insisted. If *Sleepless in Seattle* had been produced in Iraqi Kurdistan, apparently, Tom Hanks would have impaled himself on the Empire State Building shortly before Meg Ryan jumped from its heights.[5]

Random outburst: "Double-oh seven."

Random response: "Yes, and movies about the CIA and the CPA and the CNN."

"These questions you ask, they are not good," interrupted a chubby concrete engineer in his mid-forties who enjoyed "engineering films" and rarely spoke. "The question is, why are there not any films in Kurdistan? Ask the class that. Why are there not the films in Kurdistan?" Leaving aside those following the recycled plotline of tragic love, there were indeed few original, thought-provoking, or entertaining films that had been made recently in Iraqi Kurdistan, and sure enough the class was eager to talk about the reasons for this shortage.

Summarizing a barrage of comments, I asked, "So you're telling me there are no actors, no directors, and no screenwriters and that is why there are no good films here?"

"Yes," the class replied in unison. From the end of the table, Jihad then added, "And no peace." "When I was young," he continued, "I went to the films with my father and mother. But we have had no peace and no progress for twenty years."

"Yes, but it was not just film in Kurdistan that stopped. In the seventies films. Then the war with Iran and then the war with Kuwait and then everything about war. Always," added Diler.

By this point, the elderly professor of physics was worked up. "We were not free to create with our minds, only to create what government and politics said," he said. "People make movies by themselves and for themselves. We cannot make what we wanted. We were blocked."

Mahir, the pop singer, kicked in: "War maybe. But everything was really about Saddam. Everything had to be about Saddam. You make a movie, it must be about Saddam." His tone grew more sarcastic. "You write a song, it must be about Saddam, You write a poem, about Saddam, you write a story, make it the story of the hair of Saddam."

Mahir's touch of levity had set the class to exchanging Saddam jokes. No one had heard of George Orwell, let alone read *1984*, but the punch line to one joke channeled the spirit of Big Brother. "What did the man do instead of buying a television?" it began. "He taped a picture of Saddam to his refrigerator. That way he was always looking at Saddam and Saddam always looking at him. Just like watching television only cheaper." Though many were speaking freely and excitedly in English, the topic when indulged at length left some in the class visibly uncomfortable.

Just before changing the subject back to film, or at least the politics of filmmaking, I asked if they had told these jokes in the 1980s. The class looked at me dumbfounded. A handful of the professors in the class had been at the University of Sala-haddin in Suleymania, before it had been moved to Arbil by Saddam. Saddam's intelligence officials had infiltrated the campus, including the faculty. During his rule, the campus was no place for Saddam jokes. Neither were the barbershop, the restaurant, or the newspaper office. "Maybe to your family or the very closest of friends," someone offered, finally answering my question.

I asked why filmmaking had not expanded after the uprising of 1991 and the relative autonomy that followed. Jihad jumped at the question. "Art is of society. It is of here and here we have had suffering from many troubles. First from dictator, then internal war. This damage all attempts at art. I hope. From now on I am optimistic."

A people, Jihad seemed to be saying, might be able to throw a dictator off their backs, but it is much more difficult to get him out of their minds. Saddam had stifled creativity for so long it could not simply jump-start itself again. The civil wars of 1994 and 1996 had created instability and had even sparked some limited prosperity, but the shadow of the dictator continued to loom in the Kurdish mind.

Anthony Shadid, of the *Washington Post,* described in *Night Draws Near* an Iraqi hammering away at the base of a statue of Saddam as Baghdad fell in 2003. "I'm forty-nine," the man said as he went on swinging, "but I have never lived a single day. Only now will I start living." A veteran of the Iran-Iraq War from Basra told Shadid. "You had to postpone all your dreams. I like life. I like sports, art, poetry, music, whatever, all these things."[6]

In a classroom three hundred miles to the north of Baghdad, without a sledgehammer, but with the same angst and eagerness, the physics professor spoke last in the day's discussion. "Our life starts now. Ninety percent of us believe our life starts now. Since 2-0-0-3. Since Saddam falls."

Our next class was on music, and we began as usual with vocabulary, especially genres. Many in the class were fans of opera and classical music, but none were familiar with rap or rock 'n' roll. Somewhat taken back, I played "Yesterday" on my laptop and asked if any had heard the song. No responses. "Has anybody ever heard of the Beatles?" One student wanted a definition of the word. Another asked if we were talking about a genre or an instrument. Not a single person claimed to have heard of the Beatles. For my part, before I came to his country I had never heard of Mahir, who would later outdo my grainy recordings with a live performance in class. Still curious, however, I pressed. "Frank Sinatra?" No. "The Rolling Stones? Bob Dylan?" No recognition whatsoever. "Elvis Presley?" I muttered finally. Finally a knowing "Of course," in the tone one uses to answer a ludicrous question. One student was very pleased with himself for thinking of the terms that would make the matter clear: "Of course we know who Elvis is. Elvis is *Titanic*. He is like *Titanic* of music."

Where to begin a conversation on half a century of popular Western music? I played more Beatles, some Miles Davis, and their first Louis Armstrong. Though music of all kinds was increasingly available through the booming satellite television service, OutKast's "Hey Ya" was the first rap song anyone in the class remembered having heard. Unlike my guards, these students had not yet plugged into the satellite dish culture that proliferated after 2003. And to underscore my point about globalization, I played part of a new U2 album I had downloaded in an Internet café in northern Iraq.

"Freedom has a scent like the top of a newborn baby's head," Bono declares in the song "Miracle Drug." U2's iconic front man is not wrong about the limitless possibilities embodied by infant life, but in this time and this place, the first whiff of freedom came for many in their twenties, in middle age, or even in their late sixties. History cannot be erased. And change cannot restore lost years. Freedom was a new thing, but it was not an elixir; it would be what one made of it. Our conversations made clear this awareness: choice started now, the hope for happiness started now, and so essentially life started now for many in this part of Iraq.

For the foreseeable future, freedom here would not smell like a newborn baby. In central Iraq, freedom smelled of blood and burning rubber. Freedom crawled through the streets of Kirkuk, unable to keep up with the smoke from sabotaged oil fields. In the north, in a dirty and disorganized classroom, freedom smelled somewhat sweeter but still could not mask the scent of the past. Now, if nothing else, the future was theirs to lose. And so the menaces of disease spread through travel, globalization's homogenizing pressures, super-empowered individuals, and Internet porn were all issues for later. Before anything else they had to unlearn former habits and develop new ones.

In *The Making of the English Working Class*, E. P. Thompson asserted the need to understand lives on their own terms, even when, as sometimes happens, these terms are most unfortunate. "Their aspirations were valid in terms of their own experience; and, if they were casualties of history, they remain, condemned in their own lives, as casualties." Despite the violence that followed, the explosions that ruined thousands of lives in Baghdad and Basra, despite the harrowing uncertainties that plagued life in Arbil, the U.S. action in Iraq had at least promised that the man with the sledgehammer, the veteran, and the aging physics professor would not remain "condemned in their own lives, as casualties." More than that is perhaps wishful thinking. "Man is born to live, not to prepare for life. Life itself—the gift of life— is such a breathtakingly serious thing," Dr. Yuri Zhivago reflects amid the war and chaos of his own time. And therein lies the great hope and frequent tragedy of the effort in Iraq: it was breathtakingly serious, as serious as a life—and many would begin anew as best they could, while many others would become casualties once again.[7]

6. The Hemingway Lectures

Thank you for the lecture. We hope very much that you come back but I have one question. Who is Joe DiMaggio and why does the Old Man keep all this interest in baseball?

—*Fourth-year English student*

ALI, his colleagues liked to say, spoke English like a lord. The thirty-three-year-old *mamosta* of English and translation at Salahaddin University did indeed have all the affectations and intonations of a good Etonian, though he had never been to an English-speaking country, or even out of northern Iraq. This was the great reach of the BBC World radio service: not only had Ali learned English, but he had carefully chosen the particular presenters whose accents he would emulate. He was an autodidactic Eliza Doolittle.

Always clean-shaven, his hair just slightly disheveled in a rakish way, Ali did his best to groom himself in accordance with his adopted accent. Whereas the daily grime of Arbil showed on the shirt collars of most professors, and mud and dust caked on their shoes and cuffs, Ali's attire was unbesmirched by the setting in which we taught. If an Oxbridge tie from some colonial official of the 1920s had miraculously survived in one of the city's bazaars, he would have found it. He could have matched it with one of his various sweater vests, complementing his prim blue blazer. If mail service to Iraqi Kurdistan had existed, he could have gone online and ordered matching college-crest cuff links from an Oxford High Street store.

When Ali heard via some university grapevine that a native English speaker, a graduate of Oxford even, was teaching in the history department and at the Language Center, he made it a high priority to obtain an introduction. Between my first two history lectures, there was tea in the Faculty Club—a single room with plastic chairs and tables and a less than full-length door hiding a bathroom in the corner, Ali gently grabbed the back of my arm and insisted that I join him at his table. He had none of the ease or air of his assumed identity, but presented himself with impressive confidence all the same. He had, I should know, degrees from "the University of Salahaddin in Arbil in translation and English—both a B.A. and an M.A., that is." His specialty, as I might have guessed had he taken a breath before telling me himself, was nineteenth-century British literature.

The surrounding guns and camouflage, the tea in plastic cups served in the cinder-block buildings with failing electricity, made his accent seem only more out of place. Nonetheless, his vocabulary and grammar were good, and I accepted his offer to substitute occasionally for Bayan as translator in my history lectures just as I had his invitation to tea and his rather formal welcome to his country of "Kurdistan and Iraq." He was competent and companionable as well as insistent.

Not a minute passed between our agreement before he asked that I lecture in the department of translation and English. Ali's, I would soon discover, was merely first in an endless succession of requests for unscheduled instruction and extra lectures. Government officials would offer me hourly rates for individual teaching while peshmerga tried to trade Kalashnikov lessons for American vocabulary. Officials from the Kurdish intelligence service gave me a complimentary tour of the city's dilapidated zoo in hopes of practicing their English. The hotel's gardener offered sunflower seeds in exchange for five minutes of grammar daily. Like the dollar, English was a principal currency here; the flow of journalists and private contractors ensured steady work for translators, and the few fluent speakers available were in high demand.

I suggested to Ali that we wait a few weeks and see how my schedule took shape; I had my hands full delivering lectures on American history while also teaching English to the university's deans and professors at the Language Center. But Ali had been formed, indeed had succeeded to a degree, in a system that rewarded connections and persistence above all. He would not be easily put off. We had reached the point where the welcoming "no problem" and "I'd like to help" had become the insistent "may I ask of you a favor" or even "tomorrow you will."

Ali was exemplary, but this was the M.O. of virtually anyone with contacts that might, through whatever contortions, be leveraged into some sort of favor. How, for instance, do you tell your bodyguard, the man who diligently shadows you in the bazaar and sits by your car or outside of your class, that you will not speak to the university president on behalf of his sister?

Numbing persistence, imperviousness to rebuff, even whiffs of blackmail, are hardly unique to Kurdistan: they occur everywhere a few guard access to what the many want, in Washington for instance, where under different circumstances, Ali might have succeeded as a lobbyist. Ali and my bodyguard, the gardener and the young peshmerga were simply playing by the rules of the game as they and their parents had always known them. The great game was a trickle-down economy of preferment.

Despite ten years of self-rule, the Kurds had not moved beyond the constant quest for *wasta,* an Arabic term used in Arbil to refer to connections. A businessman may spend days in one of the city's hotels waiting to exchange cards with some of the prime minister's representatives. Europeans who know their way around the region can make a good living introducing prospective investors to the right people.

Etherington noted this phenomenon when trying to set up a

government in Kut: "The sharp dissimilarity between Iraqi and Western ideas about the extent to which one should relate a post to performance was striking. What Iraqis mainly sought was the power of patronage: the key was to ensure that one's group—whether tribe, immediate family or friends—remained in the ascendant."[1] Meritocratic practices remain a work in progress in the U.S., but in this section of Iraq, as in much of the Middle East, they were barely in their infancy.

And the academic realm was in no way exempt. To obtain a meeting with the university president might, for some, require waiting two or three hours while a stream of young Kurds and some Arabs pass through his office. Hardly a handful of the more than fifteen thousand enrolled students are in the queue; the multitudes are applicants, all of whom believe that establishing a personal connection to the president, or at least his assistant, is vital to admission. To delegate authority is to delegate honor, and the prestige of deciding other people's fates. The president was ambitious and forward-looking, but institutions, especially those as large as Salahaddin University, cannot change in a day.

Early in my stay, I had not yet developed the indispensable ability to resist invitations and the requests that often followed them. I would give in and visit the university president for my bodyguard's sister, just as I would visit with one of his bosses at the security agency. I would learn to shoot a Kalashnikov in exchange for teaching dirty words in English (a more than fair trade) and accept the gardener's sunflower seeds as we talked politics and the basics of English grammar. I would also accede, after a week of visits and phone calls, to Ali's request that I teach in his department. "Oh very fine, very good. This will be so very fine for the students."

Ali explained that I could teach twentieth-century American literature or nineteenth-century British novels (subjects I had studied as an undergraduate and continued at Oxford). *Vanity*

Fair or *Old Man and the Sea,* as he put it. Hemingway was more attractive and sounded less improbable in context: I proposed starting with Mark Twain and progressing through Hemingway, John Steinbeck, Flannery O'Connor, and perhaps even Philip Roth. Ali nodded with excited approval. "Very fine, very fine." The class would meet on Monday mornings and would continue for just less than three months, which seemed adequate time for the class to get at least a feel for these canonical American authors.

"If you could just provide me the books," I told Ali, "I could prepare something small over the weekend."

"Oh, very good. We will begin on Monday. And then we can work out a schedule for more classes."

Given an inch, he began maneuvering to take a mile: he suggested I take over night classes as well. "We can deal with that in future," I added in a stern voice, a countermeasure I would perfect by the end of my stay, "but for now I could just use some books."

"You mean, are you suggesting, that you do not have the books with you?"

"No. Of course, I don't have the books with me. Mamosta Ali," I added, softening my tone in hopes of appealing to his initial generosity, "I came here with a biography of Franklin Roosevelt, a Paul Auster novel, and *Democracy in America.* A student in my English class has kindly given me a Koran. I would appreciate it if the department would lend me some of the books."

So it was, on the following Monday, that I began my courses on *The Old Man and the Sea,* the only piece of twentieth-century American fiction the department of translation and English seemed to possess. It could have been worse, though the possibilities did seem limited: a simple story, barely over one hundred pages, more than half of it given over to the fight between an aging and apparently unlucky old fisherman, Santiago, and a magnificent catch that pulls him for days and nights before finally succumbing. Aside from dreams of youthful adventures, the old man has nothing but his adversary the fish, his friend the boy, and baseball. Ultimately, the fish is devoured by sharks as the old man returns to his village outside Havana. He is cared for by the boy and requests an update on Joe DiMaggio's recent at bats. The brevity and the simplicity of having only two human characters, however, belie Hemingway's ambition in the story. He takes up big matters, from love to aging to religion, and ultimately addresses himself to the nature of existence, what we are here for and what makes life worth living.

The copy of the book from which I was to teach was a Penguin Classics edition that had apparently changed hands many times. I imagined it being traded in by an NGO worker for one of the homemade Kurdish-English dictionaries in circulation, swapped by an inquisitive GI for a Koran, used by a journalist seeking to buy information from someone at one of the ministries near the bookstalls. However it may have made its way to my class, the book had been printed in Great Britain in 1974 and now bore the stamp of the University of Salahaddin on its title page. One or two of the students actually owned their own copies, passed down over the years after having been discovered by chance in one of the bazaar's discarded-book bins. Most relied on photocopies of the edition I was teaching from, complete with marginalia by teachers and students past.[2]

In this well-traveled copy, three different readers had recorded three rather different impressions of the novel, whose simplicity opens it up to a variety of interpretations. Scribbled in the margins alongside words in Kurdish and Arabic, the first observations came from a reader not far from the stereotypical criticism that suggests that Hemingway's writing is too simple, that it too often reduces life to elemental struggles and problems of survival. His characters, this thinking goes, are flat in their stubborn masculinity, his philosophy lacking in insight or nuance. Though probably unaware of this school of criticism, the first reader seemed stuck on the elementalism of the story. "There is adventure," he (most likely) had noted in the margin by the third page. After a paragraph in which the old man has a dream sequence: "The old man dreams."

Between those two observations, however, a second reader had inserted his own notes: "Excrement. Shit. Urinate. Crap. Crap." Norman Mailer once wrote that freedom was being able to say "shit" in the *New Yorker*. If profanity has a place in language and culture, this second reader was doing his homework, filling in the Kurdish next to his new English words.

Neither reader would break mold for the remainder of the book; each remained as tenacious as the old man and his quarry. "'Fish,' the old man says softly, 'I'll stay with you until I am dead.'" Keen observer of the obvious, the first reader had circled the passage and written in his meticulous cursive: "This is challenge." With only twenty pages left in the novel, and just after a second "Urinate. Crap. Shit" gloss, notes from a third reader begin. The writing is scribbled and the grammar conventionally imperfect. The thoughts, however, seemed to grant Hemingway the dimensionality his champions claim: moral resilience rather than stubbornness, existential insecurity rather than overbearing machismo.

"He took all of his pain and what was left of his strength and his long gone pride and he put it against the fish's agony and the fish came over on to his side and swam gently on his side, his bill almost touching the planking of the skiff, and started to pass the boat, long, deep, wide, silver and barred with purple and interminable in the water." So Hemingway begins the final killing of the fish, the moment of triumph for the old man. Only this is no portrait of a "champion," to use the designation of the first reader only pages later; the end brings no laurels but dregs and emptiness—the hollow victory of a worn-out man; or, as the third reader scribbled in the paragraph break, "It is a resolutionary climax."

This is Robert Jordan dying on a hillside in Spain in the final sentences of Hemingway's *For Whom the Bell Tolls:*

> Robert Jordan saw them there on the slope, close to him now, and below he saw the road and the bridge and the long lines of vehicles below it. He was completely integrated now and he took a good long look at everything. Then he looked up at the sky. There were big white clouds in it. He touched the palm of his hand against the pine needles where he lay and he touched the bark of the pine trunk that he lay behind. . . . Robert Jordan lay behind the tree, holding onto himself very carefully and delicately to keep his hands steady. He was waiting until the officer reached the sunlit place where the first trees of the pine forest joined the green slope of the meadow. He could feel his heart beating against the pine needle floor of the forest.

This is Frederic Henry in the Italian hospital on the last page of *A Farewell to Arms* after the death of his wife and unborn baby:

> I went to the door of the room.
> "You can't come in now," one of the nurses said.
> "Yes I can," I said.
> "You can't come in yet."
> "You get out," I said. "The other one too."
> But after I had got them out and shut the door and turned off the light it wasn't any good. It was like saying good-by to a

statue. After a while I went out and left the hospital and walked back to the hotel in the rain.3

It is an unmistakable if often unremarked pattern in Hemingway. The moment of human frailty: *ecce homo*. When Santiago finally returns to his shack, his great catch picked apart by seagoing vultures, physically exhausted, he quickly falls asleep: "He pulled the blanket over his shoulders and then over his back and legs and he slept face down on the newspapers with his arms out straight and the palms of his hands up." The third reader was alert to the torturousness of this sleep. "crucifixion. crucified as Christ," he scribbled, neglecting capitalization except for the Christian savior, a prophet to Muslims.

On the novel's penultimate page, the reader had underlined an exchange between the boy and the old man that speaks of time's relentlessness in the face of our futile resistance, as the will to press on passes from the broken elder to the seemingly indomitable youth:

> "No. I am not lucky. I am not lucky anymore."
> "The hell with luck," the boy said. "I'll bring luck with me."
> "What will your family say?"
> "I do not care. I caught two yesterday. But we will fish together now for I still have much to learn."

The underlining continued:

> "In the night I spat something strange and felt something in my chest was broken."
> "Get that well too," the boy said. "Lie down, old man, and I will bring you your clean shirt. And something to eat."
> "Bring any of the papers of the time that I was gone," the old man said.

"You must get well fast for there is much that I can learn and you can teach me everything. How much did you suffer?"

"Plenty," the old man said.

The marking was precise and cautious, careful not to strike through the printed words. The comments were more hurried, though legible, as if appearing just as the thoughts occurred: "It is significant. The boy can ride. The man not a master." Like Robert Jordan's final gunshots while bleeding to death on a Spanish hill in *For Whom the Bell Tolls* or Frederic Henry's bedraggled final progress through an Italian street at the end of *A Farewell to Arms,* the old man has salvaged from his ostensible defeat victory of a different order. His luck, if he ever really had any, is indeed gone—and he is resigned to it. There is, however, clarity and resolution now. And there is, amid the bravado and chauvinism, an emotion Hemingway never gets enough credit for: love.

As class began on Monday morning, I did not know what kind of readers I would have. Perhaps men more inclined to being peshmerga than students of English, who might find in Hemingway a masculine idea? Undoubtedly, some would gravitate towards the "Urinate. Crap. Shit" school of criticism, joking in their corner of the class and fixating on how many times the old man went to the bathroom on the boat. If I was lucky, a few in the class would share some of the third reader's alertness to nuance in the story.

In fact, I was in the dark not only about the sensibilities of my students but also about the size and duration of the class. Ali, I figured, would fill me in and so I arrived on campus early. The building housing the department of translation and English was on the far end of the College of Arts campus, past the never-used basketball court and the ever-crowded dirt and stone soccer field. Like most buildings at the university, it was concrete and brick on the outside and whitewashed walls streaked with dirt on the inside. The week's class schedule and room assignments were on separate sheets taped to the wall outside the department office: meticulous rows and columns drawn by hand with a ruler, and countless eraser smudges where the secretaries had updated the schedule each week. Both notices were in Kurdish.

My guards had assumed relaxed and inconspicuous positions outside the building. Ali was nowhere to be found. Nonetheless, I was probably in the easiest place in all of Iraq for an American to negotiate—a department of translation and English in Kurdistan. Upon entering the office, I was immediately welcomed in Kurdish. Three cups of tea later—two of which they demanded I take with sugar, "to help make strong"—I was led to the office of the department dean. In his mid-fifties, the dean possessed an aura of officialdom, but also of quiet kindliness. He had a worn face; the long, broad wrinkles around his eyes were more suggestive of years spent squinting in the sun than in dark libraries. There were oil and tea stains on the front of his suit and his chin fell over his browned collar. His hands could have been sculpted by Botero. He had, I was told, a Ph.D. in American literature from the university but we spoke not at all of America or American writers; rather, he offered me another cup of tea and told me how happy he was to have a Brit visiting. They had, he added, been expecting me for days.

"I am sorry to keep you waiting in the office," the dean said. "Would you like a tour of the classrooms?"

"It was really no worry. Perhaps if you could just point me to my classroom I could get ready before the students arrive."

"Oh yes," he replied, refusing to register my puzzlement. "You may have any classroom. We can tour all the classrooms."

I began to say how very excited and honored I was to be there teaching the American literature class. He continued on with his introduction.

"We thought maybe you were coming yesterday or sooner or maybe later this afternoon. We are very happy that the British Council is here to do something at the University of Salahaddin."

I shortly discovered that I had been passed on by the secretary not as an American here to teach Hemingway, but as Dr. Noel Guckian, a member of the Most Excellent Order of the British Empire, a consul general in northern Iraq, here to spread goodwill and perhaps lavish some British resources on the department. Dr. Guckian was indeed in Arbil that day, along with a representative from the British Council, exploring ways to establish and enhance relationships between British universities and those of the Kurdistan region. He was middle-aged, traveling in a convoy with an escort of British forces, and working, technically, at the behest of the Queen.

Nine o'clock was fast approaching and my most courteous efforts to dispel the assumption of my royal mission were having little success. Finally I thanked him and left the room. Authority figures could apparently be as persistent as the less exalted. Unfazed, he followed me into the hallway, beginning the tour I had politely refused.

"Oh, hello, mamosta Ian," Ali said from down the hallway, as if he had not just arrived but had been waiting around for me. "So glad you made it. I thought to ring but you have made it anyway. Please have some tea in my office."

Ali's tone of familiarity, his suggestion that he had been expecting me, established my identity—if not who I was, then at least who I was not—in a way even the insistent dean could no longer deny. Ali, he knew, would not hail the consul general in the hallway, especially not without first making proper obeisance to the boss. Downgraded from Brit dignitary to well-meaning American by Ali's explanation, I immediately lost the dean's solicitude; he returned to his office.

There can be no glide path for an unexpected American

entering an Iraqi classroom. In some southern or central cities, the class might disperse in fear, like so many drivers steering clear of American convoys, lest they find themselves near a target. But in Arbil, the initial buzz of curiosity quickly gave way to a hum of cell phone chatter, laughter and outbursts of questions; the urge was to draw near rather than to avoid the American. Ali's practiced officiousness came in handy as he drummed the podium with his hand and introduced me. Oxford and native English were apparently my two strongest selling points, and should they imagine I was wanting as a disciplinarian, he warned them, he would be sitting in the corner.

A student in the back immediately asked where in America I came from and two others welcomed me to Iraqi Kurdistan. A student in his mid-fifties sitting in the front row launched into an oral history of Arbil and its castle, which recitation I was forced to interrupt after five minutes—the welcomes were not enough; he wanted to make sure I appreciated the place. But we were here to talk about Hemingway, and so I asked the group what they knew about him.

"He was a reporter and spent a lot of his time in Europe," a young man offered.

The balding oral historian spoke up. "Like the old man in the story he was a fisherman. He had a fishing boat as well and had a home in Cuba. That is why the old man has a fishing boat and is in Cuba. He is Hemingway." One could not fault his eagerness, jumping right into the novel with a biographical approach. Hemingway, in the end, may indeed have always been writing about Hemingway, I replied, but let's not get ahead of ourselves and reduce the story simply to his personal experience.

I pointed at a young woman in the middle of the room, who like her friends was hunched over her book trying not to be noticed. What else about the author, I asked. She shook her head as if to say she knew, or wanted to say, nothing. A less intimidated woman two seats to her right did answer. "He drove an ambulance in Italy and liked to go to bullfights and to hunt in Africa."

I was barely through thanking her and expanding on the comments when a rather obstreperous youth in the back cut me off, waving his raised hand: "And he killed himself. Shot himself in his home."

The class's old man took the opportunity to observe: "But he also had a fishing boat before he shot himself. Like Santiago."

The back of the class bestirred itself. "He had many wives," one noted. "Three," one clarified. Another disagreed, "I think five." "No. I think not," the boy who had excitedly recounted the suicide added. "It was four."

"But not all of them at the same time," he said after a brief silence, and the class broke into a relaxing laughter.

The group knew the broad outlines of Hemingway's background and could name a good number of his books. They had, I would learn later in the hour, been studying the author and *The Old Man and the Sea* for three weeks already, having covered most of the book if not all of it—a small piece of information Ali had failed to pass on. They were familiar with the material, familiar with the background, but they disagreed as to what it all meant or whether it mattered, and that was actually a good starting point.

Silent up to this point, Ali raised his hand from the corner. Seeking to provoke discussion, he asked: "Why is the book entitled *The Old Man and the Sea* instead of *The Old Man and the Boy* or something about fishing for that matter?" He began by addressing the question to me, but soon turned to ask the class. It was a good question and, as I encouraged the class to answer it, Ali sat upright glowing in his corner seat.

"Because it is the old man that is out on the boat and that fights the fish," someone said.

"Maybe the man is stronger and even though he is older it is about him and his strength," suggested another.

Did you know, I asked the class, that the book was initially entitled *The Sea in Being*? Nobody responded, and a new consternation came over Ali's face. So maybe it's useful to ask, I continued, what does the old man tell us about life, about faith, and, ultimately, about existence? But to start with, what is he like?

Nearly half of the class raised their hands, their faces beaming eagerness and certainty. I called upon a young woman. "He is simple, self-confident, and proud," she said.

None of the hands went down. Class had barely started and Ali and I had provoked a healthy difference of opinion, or so it seemed. Without being called on, the oral historian piped up: "I think, like Hemingway, he is proud and strong and self-confident."

I called upon two more students, and though one added stubborn to the old man's traits, both echoed their classmates: simple, self-confident, proud. The day's second class would provide likewise united in that assessment. Either both groups were reading the same Cliff Notes, or Ali had already lectured on the subject. I suppose he had led us down this beaten path, in part, to get things started and to break the ice. And probably so this native English speaker could have the chance to validate and reinforce his opinions before his charges.

Though the opinions were uniform on the matter of Santiago, the various voices—tittering girls in the middle, the older man in the front, the boisterous boys in the back—all clearly enjoyed speaking out. And so rather than delivering the lecture I'd prepared—on biography, vocabulary words, plotlines—I decided to go on with this question of the old man's character and the book's title. Show me where in the book we see the old man as strong and simple, I said. Just look at the whole story, several replied. He fights a huge fish for days and refuses to give up. He is all by himself and ignores the route of lesser men. Even Ali got in on the action, affirming the views he himself had taught the class.

I tried another approach, asking why the old man needed the boy. "To carry the nets?" someone in the back answered, his English good enough to use a challenging tone as if to suggest the question was too elementary.

"For to talk to," answered another.

"Maybe Hemingway missed his boy. Did he have a son? Oh no, I mean that maybe he wished he had a boy," answered the old man in the front.

"Because the boy could help him do things on the boat."

"So that he would have company," answered a girl in the back who had not yet spoken and had an almost perfect accent. The answers were all perfectly reasonable—people need people to talk to and to help carrying things—though not exactly based on the text. It seemed we needed a closer look at the material, so I had two students read aloud, back and forth, a conversation between the old man and the boy that takes place early on:

"I know you did not leave me because you doubted."

"It was papa made me leave. I am a boy and I must obey him."

"I know," the old man said. "It is quite normal."

"He hasn't much faith."

"No," the old man said. "But we have. Haven't we?"

See, the class pointed out, the old man has the faith and the people do not—strong and simple. Two more students reenacted the exchange, this time reading the last sentence twice. Many eager hands went up, though all of the comments were essentially the same: "Haven't we?" all insisted, was the strong and certain Santiago's way of putting the boy to the test. Ali had again assumed an erect posture of delight in his seat, his teachings no doubt confirmed again. We moved on to a second passage:

> "How old was I when you first took me in a boat?"
> "Five and you were nearly killed when I brought the fish in too green and he nearly tore the boat to pieces. Can you remember?"
> "I can remember the tail slapping and banging and the thwart breaking and the noise of clubbing. I can remember you throwing me into the bow where the wet coiled lines were and feeling the whole boat shiver and noise of you clubbing him like chopping a tree down and the sweet blood smell all over me."
> "Can you really remember that or did I just tell it to you?"

Only after a second reading of this passage did the class start to reconsider the old man's strength and certitude. Reading it aloud in two voices had laid bare some of the old man's infirmity, his doubt. Is this, I asked, a book about a bold, strong man conquering nature and the skeptics around him? Or is it a tale of the burden of uncertainty, about the need for reassurance and, finally, of the way in which we all rely upon the world and upon others to help make sense and meaning of our lives?

"I initially thought," a clean-cut student in a white polo shirt, glasses, and khakis said, "that it was about the boldness of the man, but maybe now I think different. Maybe the man does have weaknesses. Maybe the boy is there to help him because he needs help."

A tentative gesture, but it was the first major revisionary comment anyone in the class had offered. Others soon began to recall other moments in the text that seemed to support this idea. "Maybe it is about how the old man needs help, like the way he speaks to his hand and to nature. They are all part of things that help him go on." As one or two similar statements followed, Ali grew visibly uncomfortable. Finally he interrupted a student to offer his opinion. As before, he began by addressing me, but soon turned, as if lecturing from his seat.

"No, of course the old man is simply testing the boy. The old man is stubborn and he shows just how strong he is on the boat. He is the one who teaches the boy and in the end he is a great success."

Ali's tone made plain he had abandoned trying to provoke discussion in favor of manning the barricades. The earlier uniformity of class opinion was merely parroting of the *mamosta*. My reading of the novel had proposed only to shake things up and get people to think, but now it clearly threatened to undermine not only Ali's authorized interpretation but also his carefully guarded classroom authority. He was attempting to nip it in the bud. Academic pettiness isn't the exclusive domain of any country or college, but Ali's was a regional variation, one that merged the always uncertain realm of ideas with the effects of *wasta* and limited upward mobility. It was far from his defining trait. He was polite, well-spoken, incredibly hardworking and, without a doubt, well-intentioned. People like him were going to make Iraq and Kurdistan a better place if they were given the opportunity—but they would have to play a different game to win that chance.

The class was energized by the disagreement and spirited discussion; Ali stood firm while other of the old man's moments of faltering or dependence were pointed out. Class was soon over and the next group was waiting for their turn with the mysterious American lecturer. Reread the first forty pages, I suggested, and we'll pick up where we left off: what kind of guy is this old man and what can we learn from him and Hemingway?

The student in the white polo shirt raised his hand as the others packed up. "We very much enjoyed the class," he said, "and we hope you come back again and again." Many students shook my hand before leaving, full of the curiosity bred by isolation as well as the hospitality and gratitude so common to Iraqi Kurdistan. The next class went very much the same way, introductions and mundane vocabulary quickly displaced by exciting discussion about aging, faith, and the need we all have for others in the world. Only this time Ali was even more defensive, disagreeing outright with students who allowed Santiago any weakness or need for support. Again, the students very politely and sincerely thanked me for coming to class and urged me to return next week. We posed for the requisite photos and Ali and I made our way back to the lounge to share some tea.

The lectures, he said, had gone very well. "A good success." We talked of continuing the class and I gave him my schedule. "I did not know *The Sea in Being* was the original title," Ali confessed, then added, "You know, I am applying to do my Ph.D. here at Salahaddin University, also where I got my B.A. and my master's in English literature." He would, he said as we parted ways, figure out exactly how to arrange for me to teach two classes in the morning and two at night. But Ali never called. When I ran into him on campus, he was always his polite self, even helping me with translation one afternoon. Despite the reception I had received from the students, he avoided inviting me back to his classes for much of the rest of the term. What was to have been a term of discussions on Hemingway turned out to be just one day's classes, and though I would see those students around the campus—many asking, somewhat offended, why I had not returned—I would not teach them again.

"Ali," the saying went, "speaks English like a lord."

When people here have a knot in a rope, another saying went, they merely cut off the knot rather than untying it.

At the end of my second and final lecture on that Monday

morning, a student had raised his hand and, after thanking me, asked, "Who is Joe DiMaggio and why does the Old Man keep all this interest in baseball?" There was no time for an extended discussion about the sport's place in the book or in American culture, or of DiMaggio's heroic status. Baseball is about summer and every game is a new day. It is a sport in which any man, the rookie in his first game or the utility old-timer about to retire, can hit a home run in that brief second wherein the individual is king. On that small but remarkable day, I was merely a pinch hitter.

7. Spring Break in the Sheraton: A Country Comes to the Hotel

Hemingway's army had come into Paris by a different road, and after a short and happy fight had taken their main objective and liberated the Ritz from the German yokels. Red was standing guard before the entrance, happily displaying every missing front tooth. He said, in best imitation Hemingway, "Papa took good hotel. Plenty stuff in the cellar."

—*Robert Capa,* Slightly Out of Focus

The first time Pyle met Phuong was again at the Continental.

—*Graham Greene,* The Quiet American

IN *The Quiet American,* Graham Greene's famous examination of American intentions in Vietnam, Alden Pyle comes to epitomize the earnestness, naïveté, and danger of American thinking about Southeast Asia. "He was," Fowler, Greene's washed-out British narrator, notes of Pyle, "impregnably armoured by his good intentions and his ignorance." Seductive and obliging, fascinating to the Westerner, always willing to prepare her boyfriend's opium pipe, Phuong—"phoenix" in Vietnamese—Fowler's mistress, has often been read as a stand-in for the country of Vietnam. Tellingly, when the well-intentioned but ignorant American is first drawn to the addictive and seemingly unknowable Phuong, the encounter occurs in Saigon's storied Continental Palace Hotel.

After Paris was liberated in World War II, its great hotels became virtual consulates cum drinking clubs for American and British literati. At the Hotel Scribe, where Hemingway stayed when not at the Ritz, writers from the *New Yorker*, the *New York Times* and the *Daily News* holed up in rooms half-full of military matériel. George Orwell dropped by to introduce himself to Hemingway. Simone de Beauvoir, despite enjoying a night of heavy drinking there with "Papa" and Jean-Paul Sartre, dismissed the Scribe as "an American enclave in the heart of Paris: white bread, fresh eggs, jam, sugar and Spam."

In the midst of utter chaos and even horrific violence, the Western hotel has time and time again afforded outsiders, whether occupiers or liberators, the illusory impression of being at home when all else makes them feel they don't belong. Whatever delusions one may have about being "in country," the hotel serves to sustain them.

So it was with the hotel in Arbil everyone called the "Sheraton": an alcohol-soaked retreat for writers and reporters suffering Baghdad fatigue, a clearinghouse for intelligence officials and for locals, a center for business both aboveboard and under the table, an operating base for various American security officials and European attachés. This was where ministers from the Kurdish government often held meetings. Like "MaDonalds" in Suleymania, the Sheraton—no relation to the chain from which it takes its name—exists beyond the reach of copyright law. Similarly, despite its relative splendor, its "5 Stars" have nothing to do with any international ranking system. Everyone called it the Sheraton. While I was in Arbil, I called it home.

Glistening with reflective glass in a city of dusty brick and concrete, the Sheraton is Arbil's most recognizable building, and its most tempting nongovernmental target. It is also Iraq's premier destination hotel, featuring a twenty-meter outdoor pool, with water gently lapping onto a tiled deck, a mural of dolphins showing through from its bottom, and canvas umbrellas offering reprieve from the Middle Eastern sun. Women were not allowed to swim in the outdoor pool. Folding beach chairs and a special lifeguard were provided for them by the indoor pool, but when men were present, that one too was off-limits. I never once saw a woman even dip a toe in either pool.

It was here that I spent spring break, Iraqi Kurdistan style.

There were no classes for the week, and the government had shut down for Nowrez, the Kurdish and Persian New Year. For nearly ten days, a motley group of visitors and employees had nothing to do but get to know one another. For many of us, whether teachers, journalists, or businessmen, our routine day-to-day interactions with Iraqis suddenly ceased. Young students in my history class had gone home to Halabja or Koi or Dohuk—some just for a few nights, others for a few weeks: they would trickle back to class as they chose. The more mature students in my English class remained in town. Though on the whole they were quite successful in their occupations, they were not drawn to blowing their money on extravagant meals, drinks, and late-night all-male dancing to which the hotel restaurants were sometimes given over. Goran, a young comer who had lost his father to a suicide bombing the year before and who had joined the English class just before break, would drop by, as would some of the class's wealthier entrepreneurs; but, for the most part, those staying in the hotel and those working in the hotel were stuck with each other for most of the day. The lobby felt a bit like an airport terminal when passengers have resigned themselves to an indefinite delay.

Special Easter signs went up around the building and painted green eggs appeared in rooms—a warm and welcoming gesture, but also slightly unnerving when I found out they had only been set out in the rooms of Westerners, automatically presumed to be Christians. Tables were placed outside for late lunch, and the management approved a one-off movie night to be held in the conference room. The ducks and geese that roamed the over-grown garden suddenly vanished, to reappear some days later in the nightly buffet. Most clichéd trappings of spring break—the bikinis and yard glasses, the booze cruises and foam parties— were mercifully missing, but video cameras were omnipresent. Men dressed down, exchanging their suits for slacks and sweaters, and women wore their finest turquoise, purple, or gold dresses. Nowrez is the most widely and heartily celebrated time of the year.

Writing in the early 1930s, A. M. Hamilton, the great engineer for the British in northern Iraq, recalled the grandeur of Arbil's castle: "Rising above the plain to the height of 120 feet like the truncated cone of some extinct volcano and toppled with great brick walls, there stood the most ancient of all the inhabited cities on the face of the earth . . . Damascus is a fledgling compared to Arbil." He continued, "Arbil by day towers as a mountain and landmark, by night its light shines as a beacon for many miles." Today, whether approaching from the Christian village of Ankawa or the political stronghold of Salahaddin, the great castle, symbol of Arbil's longevity and the object of Hamilton's admiration, vies for eminence on the skyline with the Sheraton. The hotel spoke of promised luxury interrupted by war. It advertised five restaurants but served food in only two. Its basement and top floor remained unfinished and the advertised "health center" and "private club" were nowhere to be found when I began my stay there. Fifteen-foot blast walls surrounded the building and its grounds. Cars entering the parking lot had their trunks, engines, doors, and axles examined for bombs. Guests' bags were inspected at the gate and then again at the hotel entrance, where everyone entering passed through a metal detector. Built into the blast barriers and atop the garden walls were sentry posts, six in all.

Arbil is roughly 350 kilometers to the north of Baghdad, but by 2005 it was in many ways a world apart. There was no U.S. troop presence, and despite the security threats, it was a significantly safer place than the capital. Gunfire was exceptional and, considering the city's location between Kirkuk and Mosul, explosions were quite rare. While playing host to a small number of foreign troops, Arbil was largely self-protecting and self-policing, a functioning example of the best-case scenario. Except on Fridays and just before dinnertime, the city did not suffer from the extreme congestion and clutter that plagued Baghdad. There was also the obvious: this was a city of Kurds, not Arabs. Fewer women covered their heads, and one almost never saw a man dressed in traditional Arab clothing.

In other ways, however, the two cities were undeniably linked. For most of 2005, the only flights out of Arbil went to Baghdad. Much of the money used to govern the Kurdish region came in a block payment from the capital. The blackouts or brownouts that plagued the rest of Iraq also afflicted Arbil: the average house had between two and six hours of power per day. A bomb in Baghdad did not echo in the north, but the decisions made by the central government could cause ripples through this city. Arbil remained part of Iraq, with a role as complicated and diverse as the country itself. It was an oasis, a place of exile, and a target in its own right. It was a refugee camp, a northern capital, a dustbin, and a convention center.

The Long-Term Residents

On the evening before English classes began, I ran into a rather famous British reporter in the lobby. The man had covered Iraq and the Middle East for decades and was deservedly well respected in the journalistic community. I mentioned that I loved England, having spent two very enjoyable years there. He shrugged off the compliment like a seasoned expatriate. "Haven't lived there for years," he said without looking up from his notebook.

He was a longtime friend of the Kurds and showed little interest in getting to know newcomers. After some small talk, he nonetheless asked what my story was.

"I'm teaching history and English at the university," I said.

"Oh," he continued somewhat indifferently. "Can the students understand English?"

"Well, the students are required to study some of their history in English. But the level is not great. I'll also be teaching the faculty English, though, which should help the students in the long run." I abbreviated a rather complicated answer to suit his clearly limited interest.

He then asked where I was staying; I told him of my arrangement at the hotel. "You're staying here, are you?" he said. The question sounded like a judgment. "It's a shame you can't get a house or something. So much less boring. The hotel is, after all, rather soulless."

While most journalists and businessmen spend only a few days at the Sheraton, there is a separate community that takes up semipermanent residence, and so must discover its soul or make one for themselves.

Apartheid's Foot Soldiers in the New Iraq

Special Forces and intelligence officers, like American soldiers generally, were a rarity in the hotel and in Arbil. Most bodyguards for NGO employees, entrepreneurs, and even some government officials were foreign private hires. And like the two Americans who had each checked in as "Mr. Milosevic," they also had a rather darkly cynical sense of humor about evil governments.

"Did you hear," a joke went, "that the Jo'burg police special forces are having their annual reunion in Baghdad this year?" Like the Saddam jokes of yesteryear, the crack typified the gallows humor of life in Iraq.

The increasing ferocity of the insurgency in Iraq in 2004 made the country prohibitively dangerous for journalists, NGO officials, and businessmen. Kidnappings became routine, as did beheadings. And so the private security business boomed. Many of the former police of the Botha and de Clerk governments saw an opportunity to use some of their skills and earn far more than they could possibly make at home. And so the muscle of one of the twentieth century's most repressive regimes flooded into Iraq to defend those working in the name of democracy and freedom. According to their own unofficial estimates, there were somewhere between five and ten thousand South Africans doing security work in Iraq. Even if those numbers were exaggerated, it is likely that at the beginning of 2005, more South Africans roamed Iraq's streets than Italians, Poles, and Australians combined.

It was impossible to mistake the private security forces passing through the hotel for journalists, politicians, or businessmen. They entered and exited through a different door, bypassing the "No Firearms" routes policed by metal detectors and baggage inspectors. Bruce and Alejandro, two personal security details (PSDs) from outside of Johannesburg, each stood over six-foot-four. Alejandro looked as if he had just stepped off the pitch for the Springboks, easily weighing two hundred and fifty pounds. These men, like their colleagues, spoke Afrikaans in the hotel lobby so the Iraqis could not understand them. At dinner, they discussed their families, Baghdad, and the recent atrocities they had watched on the Internet all in the same tone of voice. A couple times a week, they made a point of watching the most horrific violence they could find online to ward off complacency.

With his business suits and desert boots, Paul Bremer,[1] the head of the CPA until the summer of 2004, became the poster child for fashion oddities in Iraq. Alejandro and Bruce, and their clients for that matter, rarely dressed up enough to look incongruous. Security came before comfort, which meant little more than combining a bullet-proof vest with some form of presentable top. But the security company they worked for required more formality. "They are English, you know," Bruce said with a mocking upturn of his nose. He gave me a copy of the company's rules.

PROTOCOL

1. DRESS

- In the environment of Iraq, we wear clothing that fits the profile and environment of the work that is required of us.
- The best colours to choose are dark ones as they are more conservative and exude authority. Pinstripes are also quite popular and hide bulges well. The suit can be made of cotton or linen for summer and wool or 50% wool in winter, 100% polyester suits should be avoided as they crease easily and look cheap.
- Remember when fitting the suit to carry the equipment (firearms etc.) that would normally be with you.
- The trousers should not fit too tight and should fall straight. The most common mistake is buying them too short, they must break slightly over the shoes in front and reach the top of the heels in the back. In general, a good quality, dark well fitted suit is the best bet, single vented, double breasted variety is highly recommended.
- Shirts should be bought to match the suit. Under normal circumstances light pastel colours are okay up to about 6pm, thereafter white shirts are preferred.
- Wallets, gloves, briefcases etc. should be leather and dark in colour and umbrellas should be plain and black. Briefcases can often be adapted to contain either ballistic panels so that they may be used as shields or even sub-machine guns or other weapons. When carrying anything though, the golden rule is 'KEEP YOUR GUN HAND FREE.'

2. HABITS

• Smoking: smoking must be avoided. You must NOT smoke when on duty, even if the Principal does. Do not lie to the principal and tell him that you do not smoke if you do as he will smell it on you.

• Nose picking: This seems to be a national sport and again must be avoided. Avoid sniffing as this can be very irritating to others.

• Ball re-arranging: This is done without thinking and looks terrible to others, similarly underwear rearranging, as done by both sexes is unacceptable.

3. AT THE TABLE

• Conversation at the table should be quiet and peaceful, avoid topics about things that may put people off their food (illness, injury, death etc.) and avoid conversational subjects that may get heated (politics, religion etc.).

• In general, let the Principal speak as much as possible and LISTEN to him, do not interrupt with your input, let him finish then if it is relevant and acceptable you can say your piece.

• If an alcoholic drink is poured for you, either refuse it politely and explain or, if this is not practical, occasionally lift it to your lips pretending to drink.

• When you have finished your food, you may mop up gravy or sauce with bread but do not clean the plate this way. Always taste food before adding sauce or salt and pepper and use as little as possible.

4. SUMMARY

• At all times remember the NUMBER ONE PRIORITY IS TO *PROTECT* and some things normally considered good etiquette cannot be done tactically. For example, you will not necessarily open a door for someone or light a cigarette if tactically it is a wrong move. These things must be considered at ALL times, if the Principal does not like this,

an explanation of why it is done 'to keep him alive' usually
sorts it out.

A week after Nowrez, Bruce was going home on vacation for
the first time in four months. He was looking forward to taking
his ten-year-old daughter camping. I asked him shortly before he
left if he objected to being described as a mercenary. "Yeah. Of
course," he replied. "We don't just go fight anywhere. We don't
go seeking fights. There is nothing offensive about what we do."
I said I thought it would be difficult for him to leave his daughter
again. "Yeah," he answered with his heavy Afrikaans accent. "But
I'm coming back. The money's real good. And it's good work. It's
a good cause."

The Internationals: Rotund Germans with Guns and
Why Shiites Are, in Fact, Taiwanese, and Sunnis Chinese

Two weeks after my arrival in Arbil, I found myself waiting for
my guards near the hotel entrance. Bruce and Alejandro had
positioned themselves with their weapons immediately outside
the door, waiting to escort their charge to his car. Somewhat
surprised to hear that I was relying on locals for protection,
they asked how I was with a gun. That's why I had guards, I
responded rather offhandedly. "Yeah," Bruce asked, "but what
happens if something happens to them?"

"In Kurdistan," Archibald Hamilton observed early in the
twentieth century, "a shooting party is one of the most convivial
affairs imaginable, in spite of the fact that it is usually composed
of the strangest assortment of people." For Hamilton, in the
1930s, shooting parties had involved the hunting of wild Kurdish
mountain goats. A mullah, at the behest of a sheikh, would issue
an invitation and then the hunting party would ascend the
Zagros mountain for the ten-day period of hunting male ibex.
The great ibex, Hamilton had claimed, "can jump twenty feet

almost vertically from ledge to ledge, clawing the lichens catlike as he ascends." After Bruce's question, I made a point of attending "shooting parties." Hunting and deforestation had cleared the countryside of game, and so empty bottles stood in for the vanished ibex. During the downtime of Nowrez those modern shooting parties attracted the oddest of sorts, but no mullahs and no ibex.

Siggy Martsch had served in the state parliament of Nordrhein, Westfalen, for ten years and had helped establish the Green Party in northwest Germany. In 1991, when many Kurds retreated from Saddam to the mountains with little medicine, food, or water, he led an aid truck across Europe, through Turkey, and over the border into Iraqi Kurdistan. He continued this work, year in and year out, and soon became an honorary member of the Barzani tribe. He also became quite stout, and now, after the fall of Saddam, he was back in northern Iraq seeking to become a financial player. Go-between for German businessmen, dealer in multiuse crates, Siggy could connect people and grease wheels in the right way; he was intent on helping to build Kurdistan and to make his fortune in the process.

High in the Safin mountains on a sunny afternoon during Nowrez, the three-hundred-pound German Siggy Martsch, aka Siggy Barzani, was resting gently against a boulder, his Kalashnikov nestled into his immense paunch. Every once in a while he would shoot, though not necessarily anywhere near the bottles he was theoretically targeting. It was a family affair; he had brought his son and wife along and plenty of arms to go around. There were fancy German sidearms, brought by German government attachés, antiquated Kirkuki hunting rifles, courtesy of Barzani kinsmen, and Iraqi helicopter pistols, carried by my guards. It was a regular "shooting party," except that this small plateau offered none of the trees or animals described by Hamilton. The mountain range had been deforested and cleared of any significant game over the past seventy-five years.

I had been introduced to Siggy by Dietmar, an official with the German foreign service who had been in Baghdad since 2003, and had recently moved up to Arbil. Like many of the hotel's residents, Dietmar had also worked in the Balkans, in Sarajevo specifically, and Iraq was merely another posting. He and his colleague Joachim were setting up an "office" in Iraqi Kurdistan; a consulate would be too great a political risk but the German government recognized that neither Baghdad nor Kirkuk was a suitable place from which to follow developments in the Kurdistan region. Italian officials and businessmen had similar feelers out. Some governments, not to mention a handful of American businesses, were clearly hedging their bets on northern Iraq: one had to be ready for the possibility of Kurdish independence, and in any case for increased Kurdish relevance. None of this maneuvering was explicit; introductions were made over tea, as they might in the States be made over a round of Saturday golf. Outside of Arbil the preferred setting was a sunny mountainside, with rifles.

Not all potential outside collaborators were equal, however. Tsai, Dietmar's friend and mine, was rarely invited to such meetings. Tsai worked for a Chinese communications firm and had been sent to Arbil to win contracts in northern Iraq. In January 2005, eight Chinese contractors working on a reconstruction project near Najaf were kidnapped en route to Jordan. Though the eight were safely returned to their embassy about a week later, the spokesman for the Foreign Ministry of the Chinese government urged Chinese citizens to avoid travel or work in Iraq. Like many of his countrymen in Baghdad, Tsai stayed, however, and continued to travel the country without security or a gun, reasoning that under the circumstances, the rewards for the undeterred would be even greater. Like so many of the internationals, he made his permanent home in the Sheraton. He whiled away the months of my stay without much to show for his time, subsisting on a diet of tomatoes, cucumbers, and apples.

As his firm's only representative in Arbil, trying to make his way without proper introductions or political contacts, he was a lonely figure. Until he landed a contract, a trip home to visit his wife and son was out of the question, and his chances for landing a contract were nearly nonexistent. Day after day, he was stood up for meetings he'd tried to arrange. He could often be seen hanging out in the hotel lobby trying to introduce himself to strangers.

In his room, he kept a small pouch of green tea that he saved for his few friends. Generally a social visit would begin with a recitation of his futile visits to ministries, before he turned to his favorite subject: what did the Germans (i.e., Dietmar) and the Americans (i.e., me) think about Taiwan? He found it shocking that in neither country did people seem overly concerned with the rift between Taiwan and the People's Republic. It was inconceivable there could be more momentous world affairs, and Tsai would patiently and repeatedly explain the situation to us. "The Taiwanese and the Chinese," he said, illustrating the split with a pencil on a small napkin, "are like the Sunni and the Shia."

"Tsai," Dietmar said, "last week you said that Kurdistan and Iraq are like the Sunni and the Shia?"

"Yes, yes," Tsai continued emphatically, believing that we were finally getting it. "The Taiwanese and the Chinese and the Tibetans and the Chinese, and also the Kurds and the Iraqis, they are all, I think, like the Sunnis and the Shias—the same but different." Hearing I had attended church in the Christian village of Ankawa, some ten miles outside of Arbil, Tsai announced that he would like to accompany me. "I think it's better," he concluded, "it's easier to go once a week rather than five times a day," referring to the relatively time-consuming demands of Muslim piety.

The Exiles

Much of the sand, dust, and dirt of Iraq collects in Arbil. Waste blows north from around Baghdad and at times east from the plains of Nineveh near Mosul, collecting on Arbil's streets and buildings. At dusk, a man more than five feet away becomes a mere silhouette. At night, the dust is like a fog, with car head-lights illuminating its chaotic swirls. The floor of the Sheraton was mopped almost hourly but still collected a slippery film of dust; the big glass windows were covered in a muddy, runny red in the winter, speckled beige in the summer.

People are blown here as well, many of whom have no home in the Kurdistan region, no jobs or families waiting for them. Many of those run out of Baghdad or Mosul, Kirkuk or Falluja, never had reason to visit Arbil per se. Some were students, some professors, contractors, or translators; most were victims of Iraq's increasing violence; all left their livelihoods and homes. The numbers are vague, impossible to measure, but as much as 10 percent of the city's population consists of individuals and families who have fled violence elsewhere in Iraq. Much of the staff of the Sheraton was drawn from their ranks. The security officials were all Kurdish. The waiters, busboys, and janitors, on the other hand, were often Sunni Arabs or Christians. Kurdish was not understood by the staff in the dining room, where Arabic or "Christian" (Aramaic), was preferred. Many of the staff were professionals with no option but menial jobs—former teachers clearing weeds, university graduates washing dishes.

War not only destroys but also creates opportunity. In 1769, the fourteen-year-old Alexander Hamilton wrote a friend: "I shall conclude [by] saying I wish there was a war." Less than ten years later, the fatherless and lowborn Hamilton was serving as George Washington's aide-de-camp in the Continental Army. So many of those who would make their names and fortunes in the new Iraq were passing through this hotel, while the lives of many more in the kitchen and the laundry room had simply been side-tracked or destroyed. Those who had found opportunity in the war and at the hotel were far outnumbered by those who had suffered disappointment and far worse.

Abdullah was a tall and reserved Sunni Arab. His jacket stretched too far down his arms and legs, and in the fashion of the region he did up all the buttons of his four-button suit. He worked the evening and night shifts at the hotel's Internet center. With his graying hair and mustache, he looked nearer forty than his actual age of twenty-eight. He bowed his head shyly when he spoke English, rarely looking a guest in the eye. He could be seen at his most animated at around 8:30 each night, when his daily horoscope arrived in his Hotmail account.

Before the war, he had been a contractor in Mosul, the city where he was born and where his entire family remained. With the fall of Saddam and the subsequent influx of Western money, both public and private, he spied his chance. Despite his timid nature, he could speak English, as could his business partner, and they were both good businessmen. For many months after Saddam's fall, Mosul was a model of success for coalition forces. Relations between American troops and Iraqis were kept affable as General David Petraeus and the 101st Airborne undertook a vast array of public works. Though Abdullah did not win any of the contracts in Mosul, he served as an interpreter for American troops and ultimately won a construction contract with the non-profit Research Triangle Institute from North Carolina.

The contract was for a set of temporary office buildings in the Christian town of Ankawa, outside of Arbil. Abdullah spent the next two months traveling back and forth between Mosul and the Kurdish capital. In May 2004, however, things took a severe turn for the worse in Mosul. When insurgent forces struck Iraqi police officials in a series of daring and brutal attacks, the domestic security apparatus collapsed. Over the next four months, the remaining police took heavy casualties, as did U.S. forces. In December a suicide bombing in an American barracks killed twenty U.S. soldiers and wounded sixty-four others. Mosul, word on the street had it, would be the next Falluja. Anybody collaborating with coalition forces, or any international organizations for that matter, was fair game. A Kurdish employee of the International Red Crescent and his wife were murdered in the streets. Eight police officers, two of them beheaded, were found in the plains outside the city. Abdullah, with his service to Americans and a building contract with an American NGO, was an obvious target.

In mid-June, he and his partner were to meet with the project's carpenter at a house in Mosul. Abdullah, however, was delayed in Arbil and missed the meeting. As his partner and the carpenter left the house in the early afternoon, two gunmen opened fire. A bullet passed through the carpenter's head, killing him instantly. Abdullah's partner was shot thirteen times, including in the neck and chest. He survived and because of his British passport was rushed to London for care.

Abdullah never returned to Mosul. Unlike some he left no wife or children behind. He simply did not have the means—the firepower, men, and machinery—to protect himself in Mosul. Early in 2005, he learned that insurgents or criminals had kidnapped a childhood friend of his. The friend had been "a cop," as Abdullah explained, proud of the colloquial American English he had acquired from the U.S. Army. The friend was held for two weeks, and twice a day kidnappers would hold his head over a basin and put a knife to his throat as if intending to behead him. At the end of two weeks, his family had managed to raise enough of the $10,000 ransom to win his release. Abdullah's friend returned home a man destroyed.

Was his friend going to leave Mosul? I asked. "No," Abdullah said. The former cop would take a more resigned comfort, Abdullah suggested, alluding to his friend. "Everybody just says, 'I'll die in my home. I'll stay in my home and get killed. But I'll be with my family.' It's not better for him to go out. He says he stays with his family." What about getting some protection, I asked obtusely. "He's an ex-cop. He can't get any guards. Now they call and say they going to take his nine-year-old son. His son can't no longer go to school. But he has no means for guards."

Abdullah did not have any means either. His partner, still in a London hospital three months later, controlled access to their shared funds, which he took out of the country with him. Abdullah had had good luck in avoiding the ambush, bad luck in choosing his partner. Two years after the invasion, he was sharing a one-bedroom apartment with a friend and making a living as timekeeper of Internet usage at the hotel. He did not blame Americans or America for his circumstances. The invasion was good, he noted, for Saddam was a bad man. "We need thirty years to change our minds, our kids must grow up with different minds. All of the people feel hungry for twenty years. All of them their thinking is changed—Saddam thinking," he told me, explaining that he had written off his generation though not his country. Mosul had turned into a hell and he could blame nobody but Sunni Arabs. "All of the people think this is Kurd, this is Arab, this is Yazidi, this is Jewish, this is Assyrian. This is our thinking. Iraq now has lots of money? But how you change the mind? One day? The hate is the hate. I guess I hope I'm wrong, but all of the Arabic countries are like that. I told you about Syria helping the terrorists. They kill humans, innocent civilians, children. And not with bullets. With bullets, okay bye-bye, but fifty dollars for a head. For the head of a person. I hope you visit Baghdad one day, great city, great people, used to be. Me, all I want to do is leave."

.   .   .

Zaid, like Abdullah, was a Sunni from Mosul. Trained in computer engineering in the city's university, he worked the day shift at the hotel's Internet café. He was short and never wore suits, opting instead for bell-bottom corduroys and ties that ended a good three inches above his waistline. He was younger, louder, and much more brash than Abdullah. Whereas Abdullah looked like a man bent by war and the world, Zaid had the confident gait and posture of a man as yet unbroken. The chaos and random violence had not yet darkened his outlook.

Zaid never worked with the Americans during or after the war. He was nearly finished with his studies when Saddam was toppled and spent the first months of the new Iraq studying, just as he had through the last months of the old Iraq. When the insurgency gained hold in Mosul, he decided to move to Arbil and see what kind of work he could get. It was not a hardship, and in months of conversation, he never expressed a longing for Mosul. Mundane and tedious as the Internet job was, Zaid did not have plans to look for another. He reminded me of some recent-college-graduate-turned-waiter in Boulder or Santa Barbara, content and little worried about tomorrow or the world beyond.

Muharram is the first month of the Arabic New Year which in 2005 fell in early February. Ashura, the tenth day of Muharram, is extremely holy to Shia Muslims. Shias converge upon holy sites in Karbala, Najaf, and Baghdad in remembrance of Imam Hussein, grandson of the Prophet Muhammad, who was martyred in Karbala in 680. In 2003, the images of pilgrims in the streets of Karbala, their foreheads and their backs bleeding from ritual self-flagellation, were among the most striking to emerge from the new Iraq. But these were as nothing compared with the shocking violence on the second Ashura after Saddam's ouster.

On March 2, 2004, insurgents set off bombs in seas of Shia pilgrims in Karbala and in the capital. The attacks were the deadliest the country had yet seen since the invasion. U.S. officials estimated that 85 persons were killed in Karbala and over 230 wounded. In Baghdad, 58 were killed and over 200 injured. Hospitals in both cities put the casualty figures even higher. Earlier in the month, a letter from Abu Musab al-Zarqawi urging attacks on Iraq's Shia had been intercepted by coalition intelligence. Zarqawi and Saddam loyalists were attempting to provoke Shia into either turning against the coalition or else entering into open confrontation with the Sunni. No Americans were injured. The violence of Ashura was meant to be seen clearly as Sunni against Shia, a harbinger of what in the months and years ahead would look more and more like civil war.

Despite his rather laid-back attitude about the problems in Iraq, Zaid was not unmoved by Mosul's descent into chaos and knew that his friends in the city as well as Iraqis in general were suffering. His English was not as good as Abdullah's but he made himself understood.

"We lost the family, we lost the smile," said Zaid. "Everyone in Iraq lost someone. The childs cannot go to the school. The family cannot go outside in the night. At eighty thirty at night I see the city's ghosts. There is nobody on the streets. All is the white of the city. It is a city of ghosts, a ghost town. Maybe better in the future, it will take lots of time."

The elections gave Zaid a certain optimism. He noted proudly that both of his parents had voted in Mosul. "Just the ignorant people and the stupid people don't like the elections." I asked Zaid if he voted. "No, I didn't vote. I had to work."

Nearly seventy-five years earlier, Hamilton observed no joyful exercise of the franchise, but the spectacle of Ashura made its impression on him. With the judgmental eye of a colonialist, he described the day: "The more important of these Shiah festivals, such as Muharram, are usually gruesome affairs, for they are led by fanatical men who beat themselves over the head with swords till the blood pours down over their bodies." He also noticed the response of his servant and travel companion: "My servant, Hassan, was of the more orthodox Sunni Mohamedans and therefore despised such going-on, but he dared not show his face outside the building when the rival Shiah rites were in progress. Leaning over the parapet of the roof he would call me, however, in high glee, crying: 'Come and see, sir, he is beating 'isself, he is beating 'isself.'"[1]

In 2005, the holy day fell on February 20. "Today is Ashura," I said to Zaid, miming self-flagellation to make myself clear.

"Yes. Very strange and dangerous behavior," he responded.

"Last year many died," I said. "Hopefully, this year more peaceful."

"They do stupid things, eat lights and stab knives through their heads."

"Zaid," I said, "lots of blood, but let's hope there are no bombs this year. That at least nobody dies."

"It is stupid and violent. The Shia do this."

We had gotten to know each other rather well so I pushed a bit: "Last year it was Sunnis who blew up the Shia. The bombs are more violent than the pilgrims."

He shook his head at me as if I just did not get it. "The Shias are stupid and violent."

Zaid was no sectarian extremist, nor did he harbor prejudices against the Kurds among whom he had sought exile and safety. In the end, he was just a very young man who had been forced from his home. More than anything else, he wanted to meet a girl and asked me frequently if I could introduce him to some students at the university. The problem, he admitted to me, was that his Kurdish was no good and nobody here liked him when he spoke Arabic. Most of the time when I entered the computer center, he was chatting anonymously on the Internet. More than once I caught him viewing some rather immodest pictures. Some weeks after spring break, when things in Arbil had returned to normal, I mentioned to Zaid that Jalal Talabani had officially been named president of Iraq.

"Mum Jalal is my president," he said with a sarcastic laugh. "I must be asleep. This can't be true." As he swiveled at his desk to verify the news on the Internet, I caught a glimpse of a list of English words he had written down from his English-language chat room and which he had translated into Arabic to study: Deadlock. Alliance. Optimism. Resistant. Tolerance. Turned down. Negotiations. Trail. Trial. Reconciliation. Talent. Negotiation. Zaid may have had doubts about Iraq's new president; he may have been a case study in many of the biases that would plague the new Iraq; but he was also a pragmatist, preparing for the future of his country, in any of its various possible forms.

The violence in Mosul, and around the country, inevitably took its toll on souls even more impressionable than Abdullah and Zaid. Nahi, a busboy in the hotel's indoor restaurant, could not have been more than eighteen. Skinny and too tall for his uniform, he wore a thin mustache that only drew attention to the youth he was trying to hide. Like Zaid, he had been a student at Nineveh University, but being a few years younger and not as temperamentally adaptable, he had none of Zaid's youthful bravado. Nahi, a Christian from a small village just outside of Mosul, was barely into his second year when the violence—not just in Mosul but at the university in particular—forced him to withdraw. He'd been studying to be an engineer, though, as he confessed, he harbored a secret ambition to be a music star.

"Yes, the violence is very bad and I miss school," he said one night as he cleared my dinner plate, "but now I use the time to practice the guitar and practice the singing."

The interruption of his studies had curtailed not only Nahi's progress in engineering but also his opportunity to improve his English in the classroom. He cherished the dinner hour as a chance to practice with me. He was demanding, overbearing, and lacking in any sense of personal space, but he was also immensely grateful, caring, and, in an odd way, devoted. The effusive greetings with which he would welcome me back to the Sheraton nightly lost something in English translation apparently.

"Hello, hello, Mister Ian. You are my love and you are my life. Would you like one Diet Coke or two?"

"What does 'hath' mean and what does 'thou' mean?" he would ask, returning with a soda and a couple of photocopied pages of Shakespeare he had brought with him from Mosul. Lingering long enough to be sure of my answers and to draw the ire of his boss and the other customers, he never failed to thank me. "You are my house. Thank you. *Shukran.*"

In the lobby or the hallway, he would approach me in great eagerness to practice the phrases he had been working on that day. One late morning near the end of Nowrez, he tried on me every phrase he could think of using the word "drunk." "Are you drunk, Mister Ian?" he asked me after I had ordered a Turkish coffee. "Have you been drunk? Were you drunk? What are you doing drunk?" he blurted out in a stream before leaving the table, only to turn back a moment later. "He was drunk," he added quietly with a smile, pointing to an Arab Iraqi up from Baghdad on business. "Good drunk. Drunk good. But he is not a good man. Mister Ian, you are pretty like a girl."

Two weeks earlier, I had run into Nahi in the hotel's stairwell, where real drinkers left their empties so that other guests would not see the incriminating bottles by the revelers' doors—to flout religious tenets in the morning was something different from ignoring them at night. There was Nahi practicing his bathroom vocabulary. "Mister Ian," he declared before even saying hello,

"I have to pee, now. Where is the bathroom?" "I am in need of a urinal, do you know where the latrine is?" "This is a pleasant lavatory," he exclaimed, before continuing up the stairs. "You are my house," he shouted down from the next floor.

Nahi spoke to almost nobody else in the entire hotel, either guests or employees. He was awkward and shy and never failed to make others feel slightly uncomfortable. At the same time he never lost his confidence that he would master English, and was never the least ashamed or daunted by my pointing out his errors. Nor did circumstances ever seem to dispel his musical dreams, although these he pursued in private with his guitar. He was wistful about returning to Mosul, but whereas Abdullah had been shattered by the war and Zaid seemed simply to be sitting it out, Nahi didn't much seem to register that there was a war going on around him. Near the end of break, on what felt like one of the first days of summer, I came upon him reading under a tree in the hotel's garden. It was a scene that would have delighted a nineteenth-century imperialist. Eight peshmerga were huddled under a neighboring tree, laughing and smoking, their Kalashnikovs resting in the grass. As if their racket was simply inaudible, Nahi had curled up in the shade and was studiously circling the words in *Pride and Prejudice* that he did not understand.

8. History II: "Sitting in Judgment"—
Can a Nation Move Forward?

Let it not be said that it is too late to try: nations do not grow old in the same way as men. Each new generation born among them is fresh material for the lawmaker to mold.

—*Alexis de Tocqueville*

In the Middle East, the past is rarely ever just that. In the shape of the motivation for and legitimation of the present, it hangs like a millstone around everyone's neck.

—*Kanan Makiya*

A COUPLE *of weeks past midterm in my history class, I began a lecture on the expansion of federal powers in the United States. The short outline I had written out on the board included the Great Depression and World War II and ended with a question regarding the role of the federal government in the civil rights movement. If we were to have a conversation on the way free-doms had been expanded and were enforced in America, we would have to address ourselves to the role of central government, and the consequences, good and bad, of its expansion.*

When I asked about the Great Depression, all nodded their heads in recognition. When I asked for a quick summary of its global impact, however, no hands went up. Bayan repeated her translation of the question, and again nothing. A young man in a light blue short-sleeve shirt, who was always in the front between the same two women, finally ventured to raise his hand.

"We learned," he began, "that in America the Depression did

*not happen. That everywhere else people went poor and had no
food. In America the people stayed rich."*

*America: the world's only superpower, the "liberator" whose
products were now everywhere in the bazaar—such a country
could not possibly have known want, suffering, or failure.*

The syllabus for the second half of the history class was ambitious. We were meant to cover the Great Migration, the Harlem Renaissance, and the continuing social and political movements concerning the rights of women and African Americans in particular. We were going to talk about World War II, cultural nationalism, and the differing approaches that Martin Luther King Jr. and Malcolm X took toward social change. Finally, while it is always dangerous to propose analogies between the histories of different countries, taking events out of context, and even riskier to consider any course of events as exemplary, a possible model, it seemed unavoidable that the term would end with our considering whether the American experience had anything to teach us about the choices and problems now facing Iraq. But that question would have to be broached carefully and only after we'd gotten to know the material and one another better.

With forceful characters like the inseparable pair of Guevara and Hawza, impassioned though likable believers like Azad, and a few studiously thoughtful and courteous individuals like Sera, even our programmatic and not especially imaginative syllabus was bound to produce lively discussion. The students had returned from spring break in Halabja, Koa, Dohuk, Suleymania, and various villages on the outskirts of Arbil. All had spent the holiday with their families. None had left the country or traveled into greater Iraq, beyond Kirkuk and Mosul. Their experience of the world and of worldly forces was limited to their immediate surroundings, but those surroundings were no longer so limiting. Kurdistan was changing fast and undeniably around them. Homes of unexampled extravagance were going up in and around Suleymania. Shops and teahouses hummed in Zakho, supported by the constant trucking traffic going back and forth across the Turkish border. In Arbil, the airport was preparing for international flights. And all around property prices soared. Former American military officers returned to the region to do business as private citizens. In its way, the Kurdistan region of Iraq was booming. Yes, new buildings were going up just across the road from older ones that were protected by blast walls and armed forces. Peshmerga continued to stop and inspect construction trucks at the countless roadblocks. But there was construction all the same, the paving of roads, the opening of new restaurants, and a general sense of increased prosperity.

During Nowrez, the Kurdistan Regional Government had hosted a holiday party for foreigners at the airport in Arbil. Festivities included helicopter rides courtesy of a company called SkyLink. The company had two helicopters in Iraq and had contracted with the U.S. government to move private security forces and officials around the country. On this day, however, half the fleet was busy giving aerial tours of Arbil and especially its castle. Dietmar and other government officials went for a ride, as did Tsai and other businessmen. It was as touristy an outing as one would find in Iraq.

Some six weeks later, SkyLink's other helicopter was shot down between Baghdad and Mosul. Six American private security personnel were killed, as were two Fijians and two of the crew's three Bulgarians. The pilot survived the crash. Before the burning wreckage, he was executed by insurgents, who posted the video on the Internet later that day.

Holiday afternoon joyrides above a booming Arbil and, not two months later, on the plains north of Baghdad, insurgents downing the same kind of craft ferrying security officials from one war-ravaged city to another: the tale of the two helicopters told a larger story of Iraq. By the summer of 2005, blindfolded bodies in rivers outside cities like Kut in southern Iraq became all too common signals of the large-scale sectarian violence to come between Sunni and Shia. A dangerous Kurdish-Arab fault line also existed as the political future of the oil-rich city of Kirkuk, a city claimed by Kurds, Arabs, and Turkomen, remained in limbo. Although prosperity and development in the Kurdish region was a good thing for the Iraqi GDP, the progressive development of two Iraqs—one ravaged by war, the other moving forward in relative peace—also fanned the flames of separatist sentiment. Steps toward the formation of a democratic Iraq only seemed to increase the Kurdish desire for the ultimate democratic achievement: self-determination and a state of their own.

Even the internal improvements were not a universal blessing. Benefits of development were not enjoyed equally, nor was there consensus about priorities for investing the results of the new prosperity. Certainly the students in my history class were in no position to influence policy or government. Yes, as one professor in the English class put it, they were the new generation, a generation that had not "made fires," but it would be years before they might have a meaningful say in the development of the region or its relation to the new Iraq. The young are the personnel of revolutions and wars. The players in rebuilding and development, as in most political games, are not the young but the connected and the wealthy.

We considered such voicelessness in our first week after midterm. Our topic was the response of various groups to violence and limited rights and economic opportunity in the final decades of the nineteenth century. "What about blacks—don't they want to do something back, make violence back?" asked

one student, jumping immediately to armed struggle and resistance, though we were still discussing education and economic
policy as means of redress.

Guevara, upright, eager, and stationed in the front row as
usual, read Booker T. Washington's famous "Atlanta Compromise" speech of September 1895: "In all things that are
purely social we can be separate as the fingers, yet one as the
hand in all things essential to mutual progress." Thirteen years
earlier, Washington had opened the Tuskegee Normal and
Industrial Institute in Alabama. The institute trained African
Americans as teachers, tradesmen, and farmers in the hope of
encouraging economic self-reliance. In Atlanta, Washington,
black America's preeminent voice at the turn of the century, outlined a vision of economic advancement as a predicate for social
and even legal equality. Economic independence must come
before political power and the further pursuit of civil rights.

The image of the hand and the fingers translated well, but the
philosophy met with some disagreement. Somebody immediately asked, "Why if they hate each other would they work in the
same space together?" The question was depressingly honest,
but, rather than address it head-on, I suggested the student read
the next passage on the handout.

> I sit with Shakespeare and he winces not. Across the color line
> I move arm in arm with Balzac and Dumas, where smiling
> men and welcoming women glide in gilded halls. From out
> the caves of evening that swing between the strong-limbed
> earth and the tracery of the stars, I summon Aristotle and
> Aurelius and what soul I will, and they come all graciously
> with no scorn nor condescension . . . Is this the life you grudge
> us, O knightly America?"[1]

No passage gave the class as much trouble as this one, from
chapter 6 of W. E. B. Du Bois's *The Souls of Black Folk*. One stu-

dent knew that Aristotle was a philosopher while two knew that Marcus Aurelius had something to do with the Roman Empire. They all knew Shakespeare. But only by painstaking sentence-by-sentence work through the paragraph did Du Bois's meaning become clear. The realm of truth revealed by philosophy, imaginative literature, and even political theory is available to all. Du Bois himself had found it, becoming the first African American to receive a Ph.D. from Harvard. Why, he asks, if understanding and insight from these thinkers is available to all, should not opportunity be?

Du Bois's vision, the class was quick to note, contrasted with Washington's reliance on economics. Though eventually he advocated activism, protest, and nonviolent confrontation, for Du Bois the first battle to be won was always that for the mind and spirit of the individual. This question as to whether education or economic opportunity should come first was one to which these students could relate. There were certainly opportunity costs to their being in that classroom, but would the economic advantages eventually come to outweigh them? Which route, I asked, seemed the better way to progress?

"Many blacks were backward and second-class economically. Neither would work. It is the job of the government and the government have to do it," suggested one student, who then continued contradictorily: "before any approach they should like to go for the education. Many of the white peoples wanted to keep them in state of ignorance. It is general rule that when you are educated you are aware of oppression you face. Without education whites could impose rules, and education would make blacks equipped for political voice and have control over their lives."

I suggested that one need not be educated to be aware of being treated unfairly. This he allowed was the case—"Each person can know their exploitation"—but without education, he continued, "each person can't see bigger picture."

·   ·   ·

The faculty of being able to imagine oneself in another place and time, central to some degree to the historian's work, was not functioning in this class. In *Imagined Communities,* Benedict Anderson suggested that a similar capacity was essential to the feeling of nationalism and hence to the existence of the nation-state; the consciousness of belonging is based more on an imaginative leap than on any provable reality. Such feeling may be put to work in reverse as well, as in the case of soldiers trained to imagine their enemies as less than human. Certainly a manipulation of the imagination figures in all successful totalitarian regimes, and Saddam's was no exception: its efficacy in this regard was likened by Kanan Makiya, the brilliant and influential Iraqi-exile intellectual, to "the awesome power once wielded by Soviet and Polish bureaucracies."[2]

In post-Saddam Iraqi Kurdistan, the effects of the Baathist regime upon the popular imagination were still making themselves felt. Whereas in places of less-than-total oppression, like Ireland or Colombia, the creative mind could take refuge in such modes as magical realism, in which the fantastic could sublimate the anxieties of colonialism, nothing of the sort emerged in northern Iraq under Saddam. The dictator had not left the Kurds an avenue of imaginary retreat à la Flann O'Brien or Gabriel García Márquez; rather he had foreclosed the possibilities of imagination. Many of the students could not make the leap of imagining the experience, however similar, of another people. And so the question of how best a people might lift themselves up could not at all be abstracted from the situation right here in Arbil, or from the ideology of the fallen state. Not that they were incurious. Every day, after class, I would be grilled about my life at home, what I watched on television, where I had traveled and with whom I had spent my time. But the personal was one thing and the political was another—and upon the latter the shadow of the now dead Baathist brand of socialism tempered in the crucible of a violent personality cult still remained.

Guevara, as if channeling his namesake (or so he insisted with a smile that made one both doubt and like him), said: "Without economical background, like Karl Marx said, how could you raise yourself?"

"Yes, they should impose both economics and education on the people. They complement each other. Both are necessary," echoed Hawza.

A mustached student in the back offered a hint of disagreement. "The problem with economic opportunity doesn't mean you get education and can help yourself politically. I think education is central."

I asked a woman near the front if she cared to offer an opinion and she shook her head no. The friend to her left likewise evaded the question, quickly casting her eyes down to her notebook. Guevara gamely filled the silence: "You ask which one is more effective. If I study system for four years without economic backing education is meaningless. I can't do nothing."

I asked the dissenter in the back whether he wished to respond, but he wanted none of the debate I was trying to encourage, deflecting it by saying, "We are thirty-five people with different views. I don't want to respond."

After a third student led us back to the compromise answer ("I think both are fundamental. Economic or money open doors for you. Education will give you your political voice"), Sera, the attractive young woman who had cautiously read aloud King's "I Have a Dream" speech earlier in the term, brought the conversation back to where it had begun. She said, "Your whole country

My history class knew only too well the narrowness of their prospects as degree holders. And it did not help matters that what change could be observed on the ground was mostly coming from and benefiting foreigners: in partnership with the Kurdish elite, the American, Egyptian, Turkish, Kuwaiti, Italian, British, and Chinese businessmen were beneficiaries of the boom in the Kurdistan region. My students, in the relatively free and safe part of Iraq, were not without their resentments of the advantages enjoyed by foreigners thanks to the inscrutable game of globalization. And more and more, that great game was causing them to question their lot in comparison not just with their own nation's past but with what they knew of the present realities in other countries.

Such sentiments sometimes surfaced abruptly. In the second week after break, we were meant to be studying the Great Migration, the movement of millions of mainly black Americans northward and westward during the first half of the twentieth century. But Azad, having returned from his hometown not in his customary black but in a starched white shirt and with trimmed mustache, was pumped up with questions, including one that he had clearly been waiting all term to ask: "But why are the Jewish people in America so powerful? Why do they have so many big businesses and have the political power? America should want to have Arab friends in the Middle East but they just want Israel."

A young woman, who up to now had seemed satisfied to sit quietly and anonymously in the middle of the class, responded to my attempt to return to twentieth-century American history, but she wouldn't drop the burning question: "What about Judaism? What happens to the Jews during this time?" I explained that the history of Jews in America has often been one of marginalization and even persecution rather than influence. Nobody voiced an opinion attacking American Jews, but my assertion provoked some puzzlement in light of preconceptions universal in the room. Even more, it seemed to overturn a basic theory about American success.

"Well, why is America successful?" I was immediately asked. "What makes its programs and law and people work?"

"What do you think?" I countered, perhaps unfairly asking the class to use American history to answer a question that resists a definitive answer. "We've now talked about some of America's most troubled times, but also about its principles and its nearly constant change. Tell me what makes a nation successful. Why do some work? Why has America been able to work?"

Guevara jumped in almost immediately. "It's a combination of good economics and individuals who want to progress, not those who work just for their own interest," he declared confidently. "Saddam was the richest but he didn't believe in the person, in helping the person. He didn't believe in the justice."

Packed as the class was with full-time students, we also often had visitors: friends of students or deans who sometimes wanted to gawk at the American or who would drop in for a lecture or two when they could find the time. A visiting young man, a drop-in, quickly took up Guevara's claim. "I don't agree," he said rather curtly. "In Russia you had progress with tyranny and dictatorship. Europe went through the same thing. Europe had religious dogma and tyranny but eventually made progress."

All the way in the back of the class was where Ahmad always sat. He was boyish-looking, neatly dressed in a suit and tie, and he often forgot to bring his glasses. This day's discussion transformed him, and for the remainder of the term he would take a place up front, the tie exchanged for a soccer jersey or something likewise informal. "We have legal and economic and social thinking too. We have this thinking here too," he asserted, growing visibly animated, his self-restraint fading. "So why if we have this thinking here and the programs, so why do they say we are backward?"

The free flow of discussion was precisely what I was after, in order both to bring the subject matter to life and to challenge their ability to speak English. Once I got it going I was always loath to stop it, but now I had to. Here, I insisted, was a point in need of clarification. All hands went down as I turned my attention to Ahmad.

"Who says you are backward?" I asked seriously. "Did I call you backward?"

All the hands that had gone down immediately went up again. Ahmad was a touch embarrassed but irritated as well. "No. You did not. I say we are backward. I say we have the programs for the economics but we still are backward. What I ask you is why is that?"

"They have the programs designed correctly," observed Hawza, presumably referring to the Americans. "Here we cannot. In Kurdistan, in Iraq, in the Middle East, that is why we are going to fail."

"You say Iraq is going to fail," I asked a bit surprised, as we wandered off subject—or perhaps toward a subject that was always present.

Nobody in the classroom disputed his comment. "Yes, Iraq is going to fail. And all of the Middle East fails."

"In America it works, but we can't handle powerful central governments in the East. It won't ever work. We did have a constitution and a monarchy and a parliament, but then we have to have a dictator. We will see dictator here again," observed Dlovan, a young father, a laid-back student who would soon be driving a taxi in Arbil.

Guevara added, "In West you rule yourself. In East we have to have someone rule us."

"Yes, we have been brought up different under the will of a dictator and we don't have our own individual identities. So always we try to go and worship new power, instead of challenging it we obey it," agreed Ahmad.

"But we try. We will try," Dlovan responded.

Shimon Peres, a former Israeli prime minister, has spoken of orchestrating a "concert of optimism" in the Middle East. This class, despite the smiles, laughs, strong friendships, and warm welcomes, was in many ways an arena of pessimism. This pessimism grew out of both historical experience and recent memory, but also out of my students' almost superstitious sense of themselves in the world. They did not feel as if they had been chosen to succeed. Theirs was the inverse of the belief in national exceptionalism that the British once held and many Americans still do: a conviction that one is destined to prevail— another leap of the imagination. Before she took over as secretary of state, National Security Adviser Condoleezza Rice observed, "We may be the only great power in history that prefers greatness to power and justice to glory." More than one hundred years earlier, the great Liberal imperialist John Stuart Mill referred to the British rule in India as "not only the purest in intention but one of the most beneficent in act ever known to mankind." The South African general Jan Smuts would later refer to that same empire as "the widest system of organized human freedom which has ever existed in history." In this century, the literary and cultural critic Edward Said described the plus-ça-change mentality of imperial power: "Every single empire in its official discourse has said that it is not like all others, that its circumstances are special, that it has a mission to enlighten, civilize, bring order and democracy, and that it uses force only as a last resort."

The ideology of America as a land of beneficent destiny is older than the American nation itself. The Puritan John Winthrop, governor of Massachusetts, first borrowed the exalting terms from Matthew's Gospel: "Ye are the light of the world. A city that is set on a hill cannot be hid." In 1974, another governor, Ronald Reagan, would revive the archetype in what would

be known as the "City on a Hill speech." He also invoked Pope
Pius XII: "Into the hands of America God has placed the des-
tinies of an afflicted mankind." Americans are, Reagan declared
in conclusion, "the last best hope of man on earth." The theme is
that America was destined, if not chosen, for greatness. Among
the many problems with this concept of the "elect," two obvious
ones are clear: first, the creeping danger of pharisaical complacency (when I complained about being away from home over
Easter, a fellow American observed, "It's hard being away from
God's people"), and second, the resentment of the "unchosen."

Faced with America's concentration of unprecedented power,
some of those excluded from such good fortune do not deny that
it is a matter of destiny. Instead, many ask by what cosmic force
this concentration came about. ("Did He that made the lamb
make thee?" Blake asks the Tyger.) So powerful does America
seem that there arises a presumption that its power is limitless and all its actions freely chosen. When America makes
mistakes—say, in failing to secure Iraq after the fall of Saddam—
they are viewed as purposeful, calculating choices. And thus it
becomes difficult to argue that great strength has its limits, let
alone that its purposes might be benevolent.[5]

Guevara, Hawza, and Ahmad were less interested in criticizing America than in worrying about their own destiny relative to
that of a fortunate America. Look at history, they said. Iraq,
Kurdistan, and the Middle East were doomed. The West, and
America in particular, and interestingly enough Israel—where
this conversation had started—were marked for success: just
look at history.

History, however, is written, if not necessarily by the win-
ners, certainly from the perspective of the present. Between
Winthrop's first pronouncement of America as the city on a hill
and Reagan's echoing of that sentiment, national circumstances
time and time again challenged that common conviction: the

Mexican-American War, the Civil War, Reconstruction-undone, the Great Depression—national traumas that put the optimism of destiny to the test. Perhaps a sense of destiny encouraged the perseverance and struggle that delivered the nation from those adversities, but without the perseverance and struggle it is unlikely that destiny alone could have done the job. America may have been conceived in liberty and dedicated to the proposition of universal equality, but much blood had to be spilled to bring those ideals closer to reality. *Freedom Just Around the Corner* is the apt title of Walter McDougall's recent volume of American history to 1828. The next line of the Bob Dylan song from which McDougall took his title, however, makes clear the predicament of waiting for one's destiny: "But with truth so far off what good will it do?" America, whatever the national lore, was born not fully formed in its current likeness, but unfinished, in perpetual tumult, "while a hurricane was blowing." So the new Iraq was born—even if that hurricane was man-made, a terrible storm created by America's perpetual enactment of its perceived destiny. If there was any useful analogy to be drawn from our study of American history, this was it: whatever the psychological benefits or detriments of imagining oneself acted upon by the hand of Providence, ultimately, the best a country can be is what a free people can make of it.[6]

When I began, the history department's requirement that class be structured around texts read aloud had seemed to me a rather artificial way to teach, but it fast became and remained one of my favorite features of class time. Frequently, students volunteered to read. At other times, especially when we were reviewing a passage for the second or third time, I would have to call on somebody. Heads would burrow into notebooks or soft chatter would begin between friends hoping to be overlooked; but when

I did select someone, he or she always responded with a big smile, eyes full of both excitement and nervousness. They felt themselves on the spot, but they were also obviously rather thrilled. For me the thrill was to hear quintessential American utterances in voices just awakening to their meaning. No readings did I enjoy more than those of Langston Hughes in early April, when we moved on to American culture and the Harlem Renaissance.

Our first passage, read by two female students sitting near the front of the classroom, began in Mesopotamia and ended in America. Young in appearance, dressed in a gray blazer, with a thin face and her hair pulled back, the first student began to read in remarkably flawless English from Hughes's "The Negro Speaks of Rivers":

> I've known rivers ancient as the world and older than the
> flow of human blood in human veins.
>
> My soul has grown deep like the rivers.
>
> I bathed in the Euphrates when dawns were young.
> I built my hut near the Congo and it lulled me to sleep.
> I looked upon the Nile and raised the pyramids above it.
> I heard the singing of the Mississippi when Abe Lincoln
> went down to New Orleans, and I've seen its muddy
> bosom turn all golden in the sunset.
>
> I've known rivers:
> Ancient, dusky rivers.
>
> My soul has grown deep like the rivers.[7]

The mountains, a Kurdish saying has it, are the Kurds' only friends. When, in weeks past, we had discussed the movement of Americans west in the nineteenth century and the Great Migration northward in the early decades of the twentieth century, the class had occasion to reflect briefly on the flight of Iraqi Kurds into the mountains in the 1990s. But whereas Hughes's imagination stretched across the globe, in search of a spiritual home, the Kurdish flight rarely stretched beyond the borders of Iraqi Kurdistan. The question Azad had asked earlier in the term—"Why did not black Americans and other Americans who were not treated well leave or start their own country?"— seemed relevant once again.

If a soul bears the imprints of many rivers in many lands, why cleave to the country of the Mississippi and Abraham Lincoln? After the second reading, Hawza suggested the reason when he asked a different but not unrelated question: "But what about the red Indians? Is it not worse for him? On what rule or thinking can white man or black man rule the red Indian? They both from other places?"

Hawza saw no similarity between the situation of Kurds in Iraq and that of Europeans, Africans, or Hispanics who had come to America, whether freely or not. The resonance was with the plight of the American Indian, whose right to the land was a matter of ancient possession and precedence. The Kurds were likewise a people with extraordinarily deep roots in the land on which they slept, worked, and lived, a people whose souls were bound to the mountains. But as I reminded them, geopolitics often trumps history, however long. The nations of the American Indians had been overrun by a country animated by a sense of destiny, and an agenda not compatible with peaceful coexistence. They could only fight for their lives. But what if one's very existence were not threatened? What if it were simply a matter of settling for second-class status in one's own homeland when that homeland was subsumed into someone else's country? This is essentially the colonial predicament, well-known in the Middle East. It was also possibly the future of the Kurdistan region as the tumultuous, and by no means liberal, democracy of Iraq took shape. Independence had been the Kurds' dream for generations; something rather like it had existed during the decade of autonomy. But would the status of the Kurdish minority in the "new Iraq" be satisfactory? And was it worth waiting to find out? Our brief overview of Reconstruction had shown that in America the path to reconciliation was long and full of stumbling blocks. Its aftereffects linger still.

Some classes later, we began a discussion of Malcolm X and discovered that some students had a definite affinity for cultural nationalism in its many forms, as well as for the ideas of separatism and self-reliance. These were the students of bolder temperament, and they saw little value in working things out with former oppressors. They had no particular wish to see Saddam hang but neither were they inclined to forgive him or the nation he had bent to his will. In their eyes, there could be no great united national future, even once the entire Baath legacy of violence had been exposed and flushed away. That Malcolm X had converted to Islam was appealing to many in the class; that he had made the hajj to Mecca, a point brought up by a student, gave him even more credibility. (A. M. Hamilton claimed never to have met a Kurdish hajj, but by the early-twenty-first-century pilgrims traveled from Arbil to Mecca by the busload.) Malcolm X's eventual split from the Nation of Islam served as a useful reminder that the ideas of individuals, like the assumptions of societies, evolve. We read aloud from his speeches in 1963 and from a moving post-hajj speech in February 1965: "And the real religion of Islam doesn't teach anyone to judge another human being by the color of his skin. The yardstick that is used by the Muslim to measure another man is not the man's color but the man's deeds, the man's conscious behavior, the man's intentions. And when you use that as a standard of measurement or judgment, you never go wrong."

The Nation of Islam had radicalized Malcolm X, but finding something close to orthodox Islam returned him to an ideal of fellowship. A people's holding itself entirely apart on the basis of race or ethnicity was for him finally not the answer. But neither were a people to be subsumed, deprived of their identity. A more nuanced idea of culture, race, religion, and nationalism had ultimately captured Malcolm X, and such an idea was what resonated most clearly with this class. They wanted to preserve themselves and assert independence, but not only as politicians would have it. It was more in the way they would express themselves now as students, later perhaps as teachers, and as parents, neighbors: speaking their language, freely following their ambitions, honoring their history.

"Culture identifies people as different from others. Without cultural difference you are like all others. Any people before moving forward in their own political future have to recognize cultural past," Guevara said, beginning the discussion.

"But can culture be separate from politics?" I asked, in a bit of devil's advocacy.

"No. It must be used by politics," he responded. Almost everyone in the class nodded in agreement.

"Culture is for building civilization and must have politics," offered a soft-spoken student in front.

But a small woman in a blue-flowered *hejab* with eyeliner to match, who had barely spoken before now, said, "I disagree. They are not always linked. Culture can be a reflection of people independent of politics. Politics is in the hands of a few people. Art can be with the people so they can be separate."

"Yes," the woman to her right concurred, "like when we were studying with the Harlem Renaissance. People without political power can have very strong culture."

Naturally I was encouraged that something discussed earlier had not been entirely forgotten; here it was being summoned up for an entirely different discussion. Once again, Guevara offered a grand synthesis: "One of the powers of oppressed nations is to use art against the oppressors. Songs can be more effective than any army. Occupiers use culture to assimilate. So they are always related." Again the class collectively nodded.

Along with the evolution of Malcolm X's career, we had also been studying the Southern Christian Leadership Conference and the Montgomery bus boycott. We had discussed the rise of women in the workplace in World War II, the problems of female identity described by Betty Friedan and of women's economic independence identified by Simone de Beauvoir. And so it was the course had come round to the nonviolent means by which societies change. While we had read some great American poets and celebrated some noble patriots, we had also been immersed in a story of war, murder, and various lesser forms of bloodshed. But that was not the only way to compel change. Progress may often lie beyond piles of bodies and ruined lives, but it is not only the child of cataclysm.

Some weeks earlier, during the Harlem Renaissance discussions, we had read a passage from Zora Neale Hurston's *Their Eyes Were Watching God:*

> The sun was gone, but he had left his footprints in the sky. It was the time for sitting on porches beside the road. It was the time to hear things and talk. These sitters had been tongueless, earless, eyeless conveniences all day long. Mules and other brutes had occupied their skins. But now, the sun and the bossman were gone, so the skins felt powerful and human. They became lords of sounds and lesser things. They passed nations through their mouths. They sat in judgment.[8]

What Hurston lyrically describes is the triumph of finding one's voice and humanity in expression and individuality. Whatever their uncertainties about the new Iraq, that much these students had already managed to achieve. Their selves had not, would not, be cowed into nothingness. Sera, Bayan, and many others would go on to be teachers or administrators. They would play their small roles in the building of a nation, whatever its final configuration, without surrendering their warmth, their generosity, or even their pessimism. They might as yet be unsure about their place in the new country. But they would not shy away from sitting in judgment of it—for, regardless of their power or lack thereof, Kurdistan was theirs for this moment.

9. English II: Putting Out Fires—America, Democracy, Islam, and the Future

His eyes are staring, his mouth is open, his wings are spread. This is how one pictures the angel of history. His face is turned toward the past. Where we perceive a chain of events, he sees one single catastrophe that keeps piling ruin upon ruin and hurls it in front of his feet. The angel would like to stay, awaken the dead, and make whole what has been smashed. But a storm is blowing from Paradise; it has got caught in his wings with such violence that the angel can no longer close them. The storm irresistibly propels him into the future to which his back is turned, while the pile of debris before him grows skyward. This storm is what we call progress.

—*Walter Benjamin, "Angel of History," in "Ninth Thesis on the Philosophy of History"*

"HOW *many of you,*" *I asked the roughly twenty students who had shown up for class on an early spring Thursday, "believe the American toppling of Saddam improved your lives?"*

Every student raised his or her hand.

"How many of you consider Americans and America as friends?"

Again, every hand was raised.

"How many of you believe that America liberated Iraq in part to improve your lives?"

Not a single hand went up.

When the British began to think of the best way to create a modern state in Mesopotamia, the northern border became a critical question. Mosul was a desirable city for its trade, its links to the Mediterranean, and for its oil. Less attractive and more difficult were the hills and mountains the Kurdish tribes inhabited. They were not tied to the south through tribe or ethnicity, nor were they a coherent or manageable independent group. In the end, though, Mosul had oil, and the foothills outside of the city and the mountains farther north could provide a buffer between Turkey and the plains of central Iraq. These were the crucial factors in linking the Kurds and their lands with the rest of Iraq.

Near winter's end, I spent a day hiking in those foothills of Mosul that had seemed so decisive nearly ninety years before. Driving west from Arbil and passing through numerous checkpoints, we turned off the main road and traveled on a dirt and stone road until we reached the hills just above a village that had been destroyed by Saddam. To the north, green fields and new buildings could be seen along the curving hills of Kurdistan. To the south and the west, green slowly gave way to the dust of the Nineveh plain and the path to Mosul.

I had been invited by the president of the university to join him and his extended family in the most popular form of Kurdish leisure, the Friday picnic. After an extended meal, prepared by women and cleared by women but not enjoyed with women, some men set off for a walk through the sculpted fingers and gulleys of the hills that reach down to the plain. Too rugged for farming, the land is used to graze sheep and goats. Kurdish goats have extraordinary ears that hang down from their angular faces and seem to nearly drag on the ground. Arab goats have smaller ears that barely reach past their jaws—if they hang at all. I passed one herder and exchanged hellos in broken Kurdish before going on my way. Though for a moment we stood next to each other, he never once looked at me. His goats were a mix of Arab and Kurdish.

This was border country, not far from where Saddam's forces had razed Kurdish villages and where the insurgents in Iraq were waging their war. "Toward Mosul?" I had asked when Dr. Mohammed extended the invitation. Rarely during my stay, in class or with my guard, had I mentioned that city without hearing a resounding "No!" followed by the throat-slashing pantomime. "Don't worry," he replied. "You'll be safe with me."

Over the weekend following the picnic and hike, one of the hotel's many Christian employees offered to take me to see his village. I proposed we go on Sunday, to see the village and attend church. About church he was not sure; about spending a Sunday drinking he was quite enthusiastic, putting his thumb to his mouth and tilting his head back every time he passed me in the lobby. The village, as it turned out, was just outside Mosul and this time I checked with my guards and the Kurdish intelligence bureau. Their response was quite simple: not only should you not go, we're not going to let you go. Much to my new friend's apparent disappointment, I cancelled the trip and told him my reasons. He looked at me surprised and slightly insulted. "You'll be with me. You'll be safe with me."

I should not have needed Azad and Sarhang's—my "security"—overstated but blunt warning—"you do not stand a very good chance of coming back"—to understand that a friendly escort is no guarantee of safety. History is full of friendly treachery. In cold war East Germany, a man informed on his wife for over a decade. In Rwanda, men slaughtered their neighbors with machetes. A survivor of the 1994 genocide stated in the remarkable oral-history collection *Machete Season:* "Before, I knew that a man could kill another man, because it happens all the time. Now I know that even the person with whom you've shared food, or with whom you've slept, even he can kill you with no trouble. The closest neighbor can turn out to be the most horrible."[1] In Iraq in the 1980s, Saddam's "republic of fear" was bolstered by a system of mistrust sown among acquaintances. Kanan Makiya, who coined the phrase for his book and used it for his title, writes: "Nothing fragments group solidarity and self-confidence like the gnawing suspicion of having an informer in your midst . . . A new kind of fear has become the precondition for this consolidated power, born and sustained through complicity." And certainly a lesson of post-Saddam Iraq was that no degree of kinship or former intimacy could protect one against indiscriminate violence.[2]

Though the past is beyond our power to change and the future, at least in theory, is what we make of it, collective identities and relations mutate as the past is reconsidered and the present provides new opportunities. The effect is even more pronounced among individuals: in eye-to-eye diplomacy even the most rational, mutually beneficial course forward can always be bypassed for a detour back to unsettled scores. I thought my time in the Kurdistan region of Iraq would be primarily about building bonds, and it was, but it also turned out to be about addressing controversies of the past, both recent and distant.

America

The period during which my English classes were held coincided with the sixtieth anniversaries of the firebombings of Dresden and Tokyo. Reports on commemorations in the rebuilt German and Japanese cities ran on CNN, BBC, and EuroNews; they were often interrupted by news flashes about bombings or assassinations in Iraq. From my perspective, the past and present events had nothing to do with each other, were neither morally nor historically comparable. In a class where all were grateful to America for "liberating" Iraq, I had presumed that no connections would be drawn between the murder of Iraqis in Baghdad or Baquba by insurgents and the deaths of German and Japanese civilians near the end of the Second World War. But I was wrong.

Perhaps it was my determination to teach English by sparking real discussion rather than conversational pleasantries. Or perhaps they had simply grown comfortable enough with me to be candid. Perhaps it was that things in their country were not getting demonstrably better. Whatever the cause, as the months passed, hints of Kurdish disappointment in America's present conduct and disapproval at many events in American history became increasingly apparent, and not always for obvious reasons.

In February 2005, in the *New York Times*, Richard Clarke cited an example of America's worsening image problem in the Middle East: "For many in the Islamic world, the United States is still associated with such acts as having made the 250,000 person city of Falluja uninhabitable."

"Besides the human catastrophe in making Fallujah a ghost city, one should wonder at this point whether there is any difference between what the US forces claim to stand for and what former President Saddam Hussein stood for," wrote Qatar's *Al-Watan* newspaper. Papers in Saudi Arabia and Egypt, indeed across the Arab world, voiced similar opinions.

But no Kurd I knew had ever cited Falluja to criticize America. In Kurdish, *hosh* and *bosh* mean nice or pleasant and good respectively. *Hoshnea* and *boshnea* mean not nice and not good. One day during coffee break between classes, the Language Center's television showed old images of the abuses at Abu Ghraib. Standing next to a Kurdish intelligence official, I said, practicing my Kurdish, *"Boshnea, hoshnea."* He shook his head, saying, *"Zurbosha, zurhosha."* Very nice, very good. The Americans, he wished to let me know, had in his view not gone far enough.[3]

Kurdish perspective on the Iraq war is colored by Kurdish desire for independence, the decades of Arab abuse under Saddam, and the blessing of America's toppling of Saddam.

Consequently you will have a hard time finding a moderate Kurd professing any sympathy for the residents of Falluja. But when the frame of reference is broadened, the image of America as the country that could do no wrong crumbles. Instead, one hears of the country that meddled mischievously in Cuba and Nicaragua, that killed on a mass scale in Hiroshima and Vietnam.

Now, two years after the war's beginning, my students who supported the action overall were inspired by American history to find dark answers to many lingering questions about American motivations and intentions. Failures of American intelligence, the absence of weapons of mass destruction, and even the inability to find Osama bin Laden suggested a hidden malevolence that their views of the U.S. history only confirmed. As the wind blowing north from central Iraq warmed, early April also brought with it the report of an independent commission appointed by President Bush; the findings heavily criticized American intelligence gathering and in particular the dependence upon Ahmed Chalabi's tippling cousin, code-named in the report Curveball.

"I read a report today," announced General Diler, "about America and the America war in Iraq. The head of the CIA is gone, Tenet I think, but the report said that CIA made great mistake about weapons of mass destruction. It said the CIA listened to somebody who was Chalabi's cousin. I read about this guy but I don't understand him. They call him Curveball. I don't understand this Curveball."

"Curveball," Mahir, the pop star, answered. "I heard of him. He's a drunk."

As during my Hemingway lecture, I explained baseball, this time concentrating on the dynamics of pitching. I repeated Stephen Jay Gould's observation that one had to understand baseball to understand many things about America itself.

Now, Mahir was confused. Chalabi's cousin was not American

and did not play baseball. Anyway Curveball was a person, not a thing, and furthermore drunkenness was not particular to America. Still, he tried to stay with me. "Is it different from basketball?"

In his pinstripe gray suit and monotone tie and shirt combination, Goran stood up in the middle of the room and took a swing as if a baseball were headed his way. When Goran arrived in class just before Nowrez break hoping there might be a spot for him, many of the students immediately welcomed him. On February 1, 2004, his father, a high-ranking military official and KDP member, had been among over one hundred killed by a suicide bomber. When he arrived, I knew nothing of Goran's background nor of his family's prominence, but I might have mistaken him for an expat from Wall Street. Every day he appeared in one of those meticulous suits, sporting a sparkling watch, and he was always flashing the fancy Motorola phone he had acquired in Dubai. He also carried a pistol and was chauffeured to class in a white Land Cruiser. Goran was positioning himself as an entrepreneur in the new Kurdistan: he was buying property, opening restaurants and hotels, building a network of partners around the Middle East—and, of course, studying English. He became very popular in class, and on this day he was charmingly pleased with himself as he took his seat again having scored at least a single in this at bat.

Mahir, perhaps eager to match Goran's understanding, leaned back and said, "Oh, this is golf."

The dean of the College of Education, normally hunched over his dictionary anxiously looking up words, did his part to increase the confusion: "And what about American football. That is not football. It looks like war." The American reliance on sports metaphors had hijacked the discussion. Abandoning figurative language, hoping to get us back on track, I asked whether it made any difference that there were no weapons of mass destruction.

"No," Jihad answered. "Saddam is gone."

While one Mohammed, an English teacher in the College of Education, had spoken frequently during the first six weeks of class, the other Mohammed had been frequently absent and apparently exhausted when he showed up. After Nowrez, however, he became more vocal. He was one of the most conservative Muslims in the class, often exiting to pray and refusing to shake hands with women. He was also the group's hardest worker, holding two jobs in addition to his studies in computer engineering. Now when discussion concerned Iraq or Islam he spoke out routinely. "Saddam was—had," he corrected himself with a small smile, "weapons of mass destruction."

Jihad provided some background: "Yes, Saddam destroyed all the weapons. Before 1991, Saddam made them and used them. But in 1991, America destroyed this compound and many of the Saddam's mass weapons were destroyed."

Sardar, a lanky and shy young lecturer in chemistry, made a technical point that seemed to render the intelligence failure irrelevant: "If someone made weapons in 1991, couldn't they make them now?"

But Mahir the pop star drowned him out: "The U.S. government used the weapons of mass destruction to convince the American people for the war. But U.S. knew the weapons were destroyed and the U.N. said so too. The policy was already decided and so they used the weapons to convince."

There was some variation of opinion as to why ultimately the U.S. had deposed Saddam, but roughly half the class saw oil as the primary motivation. Most holding that view, like Dr. Khalid, the human rights professor who had written his dissertation on Saddam Hussein, and Dr. Abdullah, a reserved and generous dean, believed that America hoped to turn Iraq into a giant oil well and import market for American goods.

"Why isn't the U.S. in South Africa or Rwanda or still Somalia?" asked the hardworking and devout Mohammed. "I mean that we're happy you're here, we rather have the U.S. here. But why aren't you there?"

"Oil," answered the chorus of those who believed America had no interests save economic ones.

Though different from the rest of Iraq in so many ways, this region harbored the same suspicions about America, at least if my English class was representative. The continued deterioration of many areas into uncertainty and violence had said more than any American policy statement. If the most powerful country in the world could not ensure safety and stability, then it must not want to do so. And if it didn't want to do so, the creation of democracy was clearly not the real objective. Ergo: oil. In late 2003, a Gallup poll suggested that only 5 percent of Iraqis believed the U.S. had invaded the country to help the Iraqi people. One percent of those polled believed America was in Iraq to spread democracy. Almost 50 percent believed America sought access to Iraqi oil.[4]

Still, a good portion of the class, maybe a quarter, disagreed; they believed the war against terrorism was at the heart of the effort in Iraq. "Look, all this happens after New York, after September 2001," Jihad argued, his head swiveling in frustration over his classmates' arguments, "and there's no oil in Afghanistan."

Mahir supported Jihad with an argument from the 2004 presidential election: "Now America fights the terrorists here in Iraq and also in Afghanistan and not at home or in their cities. That is why they are here." Mahir's wife, Seyran, sat quietly next to him and nodded assent. In the first half of the term, despite my prodding, not a single woman voiced an opinion on international politics. On topics such as movies or music, travel or the Internet, Dr. Kafea, Seyran, and Trefa might need a little nudge but then they spoke freely. They would also hold forth passionately on Islam or what Kurdistan was and should be—but on making war, on choosing friends and enemies, they were silent. Trefa might turn her head away or smirk at me when she disagreed with something, but she would not speak up, even when explicitly encouraged. Sometimes, however, she would speak her mind one-on-one with me after class. Dr. Kafea's face never displayed displeasure or disagreement, only a certain, here-we-go-again fatigue as the men descended yet again into politics. It would be a small triumph when Seyran, with her husband's support, gave her final presentation of the term on politics; but we were not there yet.

America, the men agreed, was too powerful a country to be meaningfully affected by Pearl Harbor or September 11. Instead, for Dr. Khalid and Dr. Abdullah, among others, the more definitive events were Hiroshima and Nagasaki, and the indiscriminate, uninformed, and seemingly limitless funding of the mujahideen of Afghanistan in the 1980s. This was the burden of great power: it seemed to be absolute and absolutely purposeful. The impressions it made were no less absolute. There was no ear for the argument that an invasion of Japan would have cost hundreds of thousands of American lives or for the notion that the current war in Iraq has dangerously overtaxed the American military and ballooned the budget deficit.

Nor were there any takers for the idea that the agenda of even a great power might evolve or that its understanding of the world might change. The same leviathan that had incinerated a hundred thousand defenseless Japanese had also backed the shah in Iran and, when it was convenient in the 1980s, Saddam Hussein. Examples of American misjudgments in the Middle East were rolled out repeatedly, as implicit proof of the impossibility of beneficent intent today. The Americans were liked by these Kurds because American interests at this time coincided with Kurdish interests. For reasons of its own, the superpower had removed the Kurds' oppressor. About the slow and uneven development of freedom and opportunity in America, and any part the U.S. had played in the furtherance of democracy and stability in the world, my students were learning, but they still knew little. Of accounts of American funding for Islamic extremists and support for dictators in the 1980s, they knew much.

Over that week, the discussion assumed a rhythm and a life of its own. I did not bring up the subject of American influence or interest in the region; but rather let things go where they would. This was, after all, the English class, and its purposes were being served. Dr. Khalid, ever keen to show his independence of mind, claimed that he was aware of no American influence in Iraq today. This inspired one student to question the wisdom of a Kurdish proverb, "The mouth is not a hole in the wall that can be filled with mud."

Sardar, speaking from the moderate Muslim perspective that viewed American power as a benefit and American culture as a danger, shot him down: "You say no, Dr. Khalid, but you watch Channel 2 [local American movie channel]." And then addressing me: "And we listen to you and you are here. You learn from us but we learn more from you. You teach us American culture."

Jihad, ever pro-American, said, "America brings a new system for the world. Before there were two systems, socialism and capitalism. Now one. Now in this region it is a good thing the changing of Saddam and Americanization is a good thing that comes with it."

"It is not just Channel 2 as well. It is the radio and the newspapers we look at. And the things we want to buy and have," added the entrepreneurial Goran.

Jihad, his head again beginning to swivel to meet his interlocutors, saw more momentous changes than commerce: "In Afghanistan a week ago a woman ran for governor. This is not possible with the Taliban. She could not go to school or to market or to buy food. She could not go. This is change. He change it. This is America. We attacked Saddam since 1991 but until 2003 we could not do anything. America change it."

Mahir injected a worldly wise caution: "But America will not do anything if it is not in its interest. Sometimes we can get use from American policy but not for a long time. When we get our independence, our state, we want not to be American. We should keep in mind that America fights for itself. This will be a useful stage but not . . ."

Goran interrupted him to agree: "Until you have interests he is your friend. When you lose his interest he is your enemy."

Iraqi Kurdistan is sometimes accused of being the "second Israel," America's other friend in the region. It is a designation of which some are proud and to which others are quite sensitive. Mahir, for one, expressed the downside: "You win and you lose with American coalition. For example, all Arab countries accuse Kurds of allying with America and Israel. They say we are the Israel in northern Iraq. This is a problem. If America becomes weaker who will support Kurds against Arab and Islamist countries?"

Tempers started flaring as Islam and Israel became the poles of discussion. No longer were students raising their hands or directing any of their comments to me. Some buried their faces in notebooks in embarrassment, while others could barely stay in their seats for frustration.

Goran disagreed with Mahir: "Do you think in one hundred years Israel and U.S. will be weaker? This is the least likely option."

"Do you think America came to Iraq for Kurds?" Dr. Khalid said, not even raising his voice, as if all had been waiting for what he would say next.

Jihad said, "If America does not remove Saddam, who? It is a win-win situation. Since 1975 we tried and now it changes. Now it is a new nation."

Things were getting heated without making any progress, so I resolved to change the subject—but not before noting Jihad's use of vocabulary we had introduced the week before. I had asked about the concept of the "win-win" situation. They had not heard the phrase and when I explained it they seemed skeptical. As they saw it, every trade or political shift left one party a loser and the other a winner. Theirs was a zero-sum view of the world. I tried to show them a clear example in their own experience. In merging to form one ticket for the January elections, the two dominant political parties in Iraqi Kurdistan had recognized that both would be better served by putting past disagreements aside. My class could see this "win-win" for the KDP and PUK and could even extend the concept to seeing the American invasion of Iraq as serving their interests as well as those of the U.S. But such examples were anomalous: they refused, for instance, to think of free trade as being, under the right circumstances, beneficial to all involved—someone had to pay.

But here, in Jihad's final comment on the American presence in Iraq, the ball was advanced a few yards at least. America, he had proposed, and others could now see, was more than an oil glutton that had happened to "liberate" Iraq. It was perhaps even a nation that, whatever its interests and intentions, had now thrown its lot in with this country, sharing something of its future.

Democracy

Imagine, I asked in introducing the concept of the subjunctive, that you were an American citizen? For whom would you have voted in the last election?

"I vote," said Dr. Bokhari, the Soviet-educated former peshmerga, before correcting himself, "*I would have voted* for Clinton. Clinton very good for American people. For the domestic he makes many jobs."

"What about the foreign?" asked Dr. Kafea, a welcome female voice in a conversation that had apparently become relaxed enough for her to join.

"Yes. Clinton. Very gentle. Good for the country," another student added.

"I would vote for Bush," Goran declared without an ounce of doubt.

Mohammed, the soft-spoken professor from the College of Sharia, noted that he would have liked to vote for Bush but added a question: "Bush, I hear people say, is 'Deer in headlights.' What is that?"

As I was moving toward the board to write out the phrase, Dr. Bokhari blurted out, "Stupid white man."

Democracies flourish or founder on questions that last well beyond election day.

In the mid–twentieth century, the economist Milton Friedman courted controversy and ultimately won fame arguing that free trade could survive without representative government but that democracy would wither away without a shared economic order, namely capitalism. If the health of a democracy is gauged by participation, voting, military service, even some sense of civic responsibility, the democracy in Iraqi Kurdistan was off to a reasonably good start. If a system's long-term prospects are tied to transparency and, as Friedman suggested, to the expansion of competition and opportunity, there was reason to worry about Kurdistan.

Free-market traditions seemed to lag behind democratic traditions. It was difficult to pinpoint exactly what business the Barzani family was in, but whenever Korek, the lone mobile-phone service in Arbil, went down, as it did frequently, everyone held the Barzanis to blame. When a hotel was criticized as too expensive or the quality of Kurdistan television mocked as second-rate, the name Barzani was mentioned. The people of Iraqi Kurdistan always assumed that those who pulled the strings of government pulled those of commerce as well, and mostly they were right—though not entirely.

Azad, a wealthy businessman, showed up at perhaps two-thirds of the class meetings—too busy, he always insisted, at this moment of unprecedented opportunity. He ran a construction company as well as a concrete plant and arrived at the Language Center in a 2005 Land Cruiser with a driver and security. The protection, he told me one day, was not for his person but for his money. There was no bank in Arbil, none that could be trusted anyway, and so Azad was forced to keep all of his earnings in his house. What he lacked in political connections, he had made up for in hustle. This was reflected in his approach to business.[5]

"It would be good you control your business yourself. This is good," he said, criticizing the government's hand in distributing contracts.

If Azad worried about government intervention, others in the class seemed to have developed a fear of monopolies and corporations running rampant. The physics professor said, "In my opinion it is better if there are some rules for businessmen and if there is competition. If there is only one product you must buy it, you can only choose the one."

Most in class agreed with that logic. So I pushed the two Soviet-educated professors to dispute it. Nobody would deny that competition is good, I said in the hopes of smoking them out. But neither responded. Tired of playing possum, I looked down the table and asked, "Weren't you educated in the Soviet Union?"

"Yeah," the dean of the Education College answered dismissively for the pair of them. "So what? We are not here as communists."

After such heated discussion of American motivations in the war, I couldn't believe this was all the group could offer on capitalism, corruption, and business opportunity. Every day in my classroom, in the bazaar, in the tea shops, I had heard complaints about the lack of economic opportunity, but the words came with a certain resignation, not with the fervent hope or despair that emerged in conversations concerning history and politics. Of course, there was one benefit to most of my students' limited income: nobody was suffering under an unfair tax burden. Reviewing vocabulary relating to government, I had introduced the notions of progressive and regressive taxation, but neither was particularly relevant to my students. Sure, they paid taxes, they asserted collectively, but nobody could tell me how much or to whom. Still, there was no shortage of opinions on the appropriate way for government to collect revenue, and these opinions correlated with relative income and what one could very roughly call class.

"I don't think the rich pay more. We all make money right. Then we all pay the same," Azad declared abruptly, as if panicked at the thought of the government knocking down his door tomorrow to take his construction and concrete profits.

Mohammed, the hardworking computer engineer, and apparently a proponent of thrift, proposed the concept of a consumption tax. "How many houses has a man? I think we all need our houses to have one house. But after the one house you should pay for the ones that you don't need."

A professor of biology new to the class saw taxation in broader terms that would have pleased Milton Friedman: "No, if you tax money more, the ones who make money can't put it in banks and we need the banks and the money to start business."

Azad had listened intently as more and more signed on to Mohammed's consumption tax proposal. He had found his tax haven in his mattress, but a man's home, he wanted the others to know, was more than his ATM. And one man's luxury was another's necessity: "It is normal to need more than the one house. It's not always extra. My friend, many of my friends, they have four wives and they need the four houses. If I have four wives I should not have to pay the taxes for the four houses. When I have much money and want more houses I can just take more wives."

The next class would bring to light a problem that plagues many of the region's countries. In lands with great natural-resource wealth, with no need to tax the people to pay for government, how can the governed possibly hold their leaders to account? Tell me, I asked the group, how many oil-rich countries can you name with functioning democracies? The "curse of oil" had gained widespread attention immediately before and after the coalition forces entered the country as the potential for democracy in Iraq was debated in newspapers, magazines, and books throughout the West. If mismanaged, Iraqi Kurdistan's expected oil boom could lead to the stillbirth of the region's young democracy. Our comfort level as a class was high enough that I hazarded to suggest, for the sake of debate, that maybe the Kurds did not need oil wealth. At first the class looked bewildered, but then it quickly signed on to the intellectual exercise of considering the hypothetical. Each one took the role of oil minister, urban planner, or fervent patriot; their every answer to the question of how to spend the money centered on the general improvement of Kurdistan and Iraq. Each idea was big in scope and vague in vision, and carried a hint of understanding that daily habits of work and living were bound to change.[6]

"We must use oil for development. For constant projects," suggested one student, who spoke as if his backyard might turn out to be another Dubai.

Dr. Kafea agreed, optimistically believing that a government could be founded to manage the oil. "We Kurds need to establish good democratic regime to spend this money."

The soft-spoken professor of physics—dressed, as always, in his light brown suit and slightly torn sweater-vest—was on to something more personal than public works: "We don't need the oil or the money"—not wealth for its own sake. "We want the happiness. We dream of the house and to travel. Not the oil."

"We want our land. The Kirkuk land. It's the point," Jihad said in agreement.

"We want the oil," exclaimed Dr. Kafea summarily, not missing a beat.

The professor of physics was now gesticulating with his pen and his glasses, more impassioned than he had seemed all term. Again he argued for the individual's aspirations. If these could be achieved with oil, the oil should be used to realize them. "Some people said America came for oil. That's not bad. I can't use it. I can't use this pen; you take it and write. You take the oil but teach us to read and write."

Jihad, while interested in a better life for the individual, was wary of the corrupting influence of black gold. He advocated opportunity but not idleness. "We'll work better now. Do not just give the oil to the people."

Goran again jumped in, essentially concurring that wealth for its own sake was of no use; it was needed to bring his people into the global economy. "If we're rich and we can't go anywhere, what's the point? We know nothing of the world. We know nothing of the world. What's the point? No point."

"It's very simple," he continued. "You take the money and then take all the Iraqi people and ship them out into the world and they come back and make it better themselves. What's our role? What are our imports? We need that oil for the money. We can consult Americans but we must try to build our country ourselves."

Islam

While Abu Musab al-Zarqawi continued to wage war across Iraq throughout the spring, killing many Americans but many more Iraqis, maiming and murdering them at job sites, in markets, at funerals, and in mosques, it became easy to forget that his mayhem against civilians had a publicly declared objective: a pre-emptive war against the democracy promised by the January elections. Zarqawi's rhetoric provided fodder for an ongoing discussion as to the compatibility of Islam and democracy.

"Conservative, state-centered Islamists are vigorous defenders of a rule of law, but they understand law as divine law and see any form of democracy as corruptive of it," wrote Mahmood Mamdani in *Good Muslim, Bad Muslim.* Bernard Lewis has explained the ways in which some of the traditions of Islamic societies can impair democracy today. "The idea of a people participating not just in the choice of a ruler but in the conduct of government, is not part of traditional Islam," he wrote. "To this day, there is no word in Arabic corresponding to 'citizen.'" Others have attributed the limited success of democracy in the Middle East—from Egypt in the 1920s to Iran in the mid-1940s—to be the result of postcolonial dynamics more than anything linked directly to Islam. Sayyid Qutb, one of the founders of Egypt's hugely influential Muslim Brotherhood, dismissed "Islamic Democracy" as a vulgar and irreligious attempt to appease "people's desires." The views of Lewis and the doctrines of Qutb, however, are not without their challengers, both inside and outside of Islam. Iraqi exiles in London and elsewhere, for instance, had started journals encouraging a modern merging of Islam and democratic traditions. And so the question needed to be asked: If Zarqawi was waging war on democracy as contrary to Islam, what, other than violence, did he have to propose as a model for the government in Iraq and other countries in the greater Middle East?[7]

One of the great failures of the Bush administration was its inability to anticipate the evils and ugliness of which people thrust into a violent legal vacuum are capable. As authority disappears, and looting and chaos take on lives of their own, even good people are swept in. And this applies to both the occupiers and the occupied. Amid violence, far from home, and lacking strong leadership, American soldiers did horrific things at Abu Ghraib. We do, for the most part, hold individuals accountable for their own actions. Yet it is a basic job of government to create the circumstances wherein we are led by our better selves.

If the Bush administration was fatally naive about some negative human capacities, it was also refreshingly optimistic about some positive ones. Freedom is no one people's right exclusively; and its opportunities should be available to all. Radical, idealistic, and—to many—woefully ignorant of the ways of other cultures, the Bush doctrine had at its core a fundamentally empowering notion of what people could do if given the chance. The oppressed were but so many liberal (small *l*) democrats (small *d*) yearning to breathe free. But this theory failed to imagine the alternative logic of an Islamic social order, even in the extreme form espoused by the exponent of violent extremism, Zarqawi. In 2005, the former intelligence czar Richard Clarke summed up the Islamist social vision:

> Beyond Iraq, in the greater Muslim world, opposing democracy is not uppermost in the mind of Al Qaeda or the larger jihadist network. (In Saudi Arabia, for example, Al Qaeda wants the monarchy replaced by a more democratic government.) Radical Islamists are ultimately seeking to create something orthogonal to our model of democracy. They are fighting to create a theocracy or, in their vernacular, a caliphate.

As our discussions about travel and movies and music had shown, Mahir, Seyran, Goran, and their classmates had so far lived circumscribed lives. Their capacity to envision what a people *could do* hinged on the previously unimaginable condition of Saddam's falling, before which life was defined by what one couldn't do: tell that joke, go to that country, afford that appliance. If, as Jihad had suggested months earlier, life was really beginning anew, the management of oil wealth or tax policy—however crucial they were to the success of Iraqi Kurdistan—were nonetheless still in the realm of the purely hypothetical, and mostly still beyond the class's concern. Somewhat similarly, though almost all in class had been proud of the recent vote and of the Kurdish democracy that, for all its failings and limitations, was nearing its tenth anniversary, none seemed to regard the question of Islam's compatibility with democracy to be worthy of much discussion. They wanted democracy, whatever that meant exactly. They were Muslims. It was as simple as that.[8]

As had happened with the topic of globalization, these preconceptions met with limited interest here. Taxes, oil, and the question of democracy are big issues among the intelligentsia when they consider the future of the Middle East, and so I had assumed these issues would surely be hot topics for discussion here. But I had erred in thinking in terms of a society rather than in terms of individual lives—here it was not a matter of "we the people" but of the individual teacher or student or businessman. As individuals, they had impressive and interesting ideas, yet their concerns were pragmatic, and they had not yet assimilated the luxury of abstraction that attends self-determination. For now it was well to be reminded that during the winter, water for washing your hands for prayer can be cold and that there isn't always enough money in your pocket for going to the store.

The weather was improving inside as well as outside: friendships were forming within the group, and classroom sessions had

become fluid. Our conversations were less structured, less con-
strained by vocabulary or unfamiliarity with one another. Yes,
the elder Mohammed, of the College of Sharia, still rose to greet
every student as he or she arrived at class, regardless of what I or
anybody else might be saying at the moment. Now, however, he
did so with the kind of heartfelt smile that comes from knowing
just a bit about somebody's life.

Discussions that began in the classroom were now regularly
continuing over tea and coffee or out on the street. While
democracy's relation to Islam still sparked little interest, the
place of Islam in the individual's life was a recurrent and fiercely
debated theme. And I was not usually the one who brought it
up. It was now just weeks before the end of term, and people
who otherwise would never have come to know one another—
whether because of differences in age, gender, or wealth—had
reached the point of comfortably disagreeing about sensitive
subjects.

The younger Mohammed, the one with conservative views and
too many jobs, had arrived for afternoon class on this mid-April
day with a gift for me: a Koran. It was the third I had received, all
finely bound and colored editions printed by an Islamic group in
Cairo and sold in the bazaar. It was a gesture of hospitality, gratitude, and friendship—Mohammed wanted to share with me that
which was most important to him. Nonetheless, some in the
class took immediate exception to his choice of gift.

"Give him something from Kurdish culture, not Islam,"
Goran said.

Mohammed responded without a moment's hesitation: "No.
We must have some Islamic culture as well. Not just praying.
This is part of Islamic culture."

"No. Islamic culture is Arab culture," Goran replied, making
clear that a debate about the place of Islam in Iraqi Kurdistan
was also a debate about Arab influence.

Mahir had arrived early, without Seyran, and quickly joined the discussion. "Arab has no culture," he declared. "It's just beheading and tell your woman to stay home."

The conversation appeared to be descending into an anti-Arab diatribe, and though I wanted to return to the original topic, I could not force them—it was their religion, their culture, and we were not yet in the classroom. "Arabs just take from our culture and we lose some. Like Salahaddin. Have you seen his tomb in Damascus? It says he has a Kurdish mother, not that he is Kurdish," Goran continued. "They take him and us. We must protect our culture."

Gesticulating vaguely toward the Koran I was holding, Mohammed, now excited and defensive, started stammering in English. "We don't need Islam to—no—for . . . We don't need Islam just for praying."

"Yes. Just for praying," Goran quickly replied.

Jihad had been sitting quietly on one of the grandiose imitation-nineteenth-century couches in the reception area where we had gathered. The kitchen at the Language Center was staffed almost entirely by Yazidis, members of a small religious group often misunderstood to be fire worshippers, whose rather secretive theology combines elements of Zoroastrianism, Judaism, Christianity, and Islam. They soon left their work and joined the discussion, knowing no English, but commenting among themselves on the general excitement. For Jihad, this was a long time to remain silent.

He took it upon himself to retreat from efforts to find a middle ground, and went immediately after Mohammed. "Do you want an Islamic state?"

"Of course not," Mohammed responded.

"Like Saudi Arabia where the woman can do nothing," Jihad said, continuing the offensive.

Debates about the role of Islam in the new government were taking place all over Iraq. Here, in the capital of the Kurdistan region, the question had an additional complexity. For although Saddam had been a secularist until the 1990s, he and his regime were Arab; and Islam was an Arab phenomenon, at least in origin—although now it was also the Kurds' religion. In Kurdistan, where I had heard it said repeatedly that Iraq was doomed simply because of what had happened to the Kurds before the toppling of Saddam, Islam inspired a somewhat similar pessimism. When one imagined its influence in the new government, one imagined more Arab influence.

"Islam has been used as a card by the Arabs and the Turks, and the Kurds have been oppressed by this card," Mahir stated.

Mohammed smiled and nodded in agreement. They had, it seemed to this devout Muslim, finally gotten the point. "We should fight Arabs by Islam. We must make Islam our own. We always use it for Arabs. We must use it for ourselves and we can use it against them." To this Goran, Jihad, and Mahir could all agree.

Soon afterward, now in the classroom, an argument started over the Islamic tenet of jihad. Obviously various sects and clerics differed, but what exactly was its proper place in the faith?

"At the center of Islam is jihad," suggested Dr. Bokhari.

"Yes," answered an older man. "But if you pay someone to kill themselves, where is the jihad in that?" "It is not Muslim. Osama bin Laden is not a Muslim."

"He says that *you* are not a Muslim," the political scientist replied. "Who is to say which is right?"

"We are," responded Mohammed the pious, whose indignation was echoed by the rest of the class, "and we know bin Laden is wrong."

Until that moment, I had not heard ordinary Muslims in the Middle East speak out vehemently and sincerely to disown what had been done in the name of their faith. I also hadn't realized how much I needed to hear it.

Back to the Future

As the term approached its end, I began to wonder just how much self-awareness existed among these highly opinionated and colorful students of mine. Did they understand the limitations that years in suspended animation had inflicted upon them? Would they be up to seeing their country through to a new political system or were they destined to be mainly victims of history, a "lost generation," smart, good, and caring people but a bit too old for new tricks?

The new age in Iraq and Kurdistan, as Jihad reminded me, had started in their minds only after the capture of Saddam Hussein. "From 1991, always we were afraid he would come back or make agreement with other countries. We can progress great now. But we can't then. Not until he is destroyed." They did not have long to wait.

Mohammed, who had given me the Koran, agreed. "We not believe in our new period until the liberation of Iraq. The fall of Saddam's regime. And now with new period we must start reshaping."

Goran described the struggles of the government and the people in the mid-1990s: "At first democracy was you could just do anything. You didn't answer to anyone. But now we get better. And we all begin to have people outside in Europe and America and they tell us and they send money. They make real difference." That the flow of remittances from the Kurdish diaspora should have counted for so much was an apt reminder that political freedom was only half the challenge. Free markets do not merely crop up like weeds, whatever the most militant advocate of laissez-faire may think. A certain amount of seeding and cultivation is necessary.

Bahadin was the son of a now elderly Iranian peshmerga who had been trained only for fighting and who supported his family on a thirty-dollar-per-month pension. Bahadin was studying medicine at the university; he was the first in his family to complete the equivalent of high school. His father, the son allowed, could not make sense of all this education, and Bahadin himself was quick to acknowledge the lingering self-defeating consequences of a people having schooled generation after generation in war rather than reading. "We take all the men from their schools and stores and wives and families and tell them to go to the mountain and fight. They come back and everything is changed and they can't do. They go the mountains and then have nothing. They can't do anything now."9

"Yes, we have enemies in the government in Syria, in Turkey, in Iran," Jihad responded, "but we also have our own enemies in our head."

How do you fight those enemies? I asked. Who leads that fight? "From the youth," Mahir answered simply.

Clearly moved by the thought of the straitened circumstances of his father's life, Bahadin nonetheless tried to follow the shift in conversation. "We're used to living under authority and—"

Goran interrupted him: "Not making the decisions. The authority made the decisions. . . . Our mental level is not higher now. We learn to identify good things and bad things. We are like a child, from dark to light. We are beginning in democracy and we need information as well as the law." Pointing to his head, he concluded, "Here knowledge is just as important."10

Dr. Kafea, well into her late fifties, was more succinct and more resigned: "After this, after ours, theirs is the new generation that can make this democracy. Not us."

Even the relatively young and indefatigably entrepreneurial Goran had to concede demographic realities to a degree: "They know more about democracy. They even have different clothes. They have some English. They are better," he allowed a little mournfully.

10. Battles in the Universities

Goodness without knowledge is weak . . . yet knowledge
without goodness is dangerous.

*—1778 Constitution of Phillips Academy Andover,
prep school of George W. Bush and Paul Bremer*

IN 1258, when the Mongols conquered Baghdad, they rolled
the last Abbasid caliph up in a carpet before trampling him to
death to prevent his royal blood from being spilled on the
ground. The blood of others stained the ground, however, and
plenty of it: victims numbered in the thousands, and legend has
it that the water of the River Tigris ran red. According to similar
authority, they later ran black with the ink from the great capital's countless drowned books.

On April 6, 2003, a battle group of the First United Kingdom
Armored Division laid siege to Basra's College of Literature,
where three hundred Islamic fighters from Syria as well as countries in North Africa had established themselves. After secur-
ing the buildings and expelling the irregulars, the main body of
the First Armored Division set up headquarters on campus.
Baghdad had fallen just the day before, and, within the week, the
capital's universities were looted.[1]

On a Monday in September 2005, gunmen dressed as Sunni
Arab fighters entered the Jazeera primary school in a Sunni Arab
suburb of Baghdad, forcing five teachers and a driver into a
room, where the gunmen shot and killed them. The *New York
Times* reported that many children were still at school when the
gunmen entered the building at 1:15 in the afternoon.

The U.S.-led effort in Iraq was not meant merely to topple

but to supplant an existing order. Just as a democracy would need to be built brick by brick where Saddam's edifice of repression had stood, every desk and book destroyed in war would have to be replaced. Every schoolroom looted after the fall of Baghdad needed to be refurnished in the rebuilding process.

In February 2005, a United Nations report found that 84 percent of Iraq's higher education infrastructure had been damaged in the war and subsequent looting. Once among the finest in the Middle East—those in Baghdad and Mosul were especially distinguished—the nation's universities had been deteriorating since the Iran-Iraq War. The financial drain of the war against Iran and the invasion of Kuwait, coupled with political oppression and intellectual isolation, took a heavy toll on the facilities and their faculties. After the First Gulf War, 30 to 40 percent of the country's professors had fled for jobs in Europe and North America. The intellectual isolation would end with the fall of Saddam, but the professors would face new pressures, and the brain drain would continue. According to the Association of University Teachers, 2,000 professors left the country between the start of the latest war and the end of 2004. In Mosul and in Baghdad, as elsewhere in Iraq, lecturers were gunned down, some on the street, some in their cars, some in the classroom. A UNESCO conference in Paris at the beginning of 2005, which included representatives from many of Iraq's universities, found that at least forty-seven professors had been assassinated between Saddam's fall and the beginning of 2005, but other sources held that as many as three hundred professors, academics, and administrators had been killed in that same time frame.[2]

John Agresto, who oversaw the country's university system for the Coalition Provisional Authority beginning in 2003, concluded that the campuses around the country needed $1.2 billion to rebuild and modernize. In a reconstruction aid budget approved in 2003, the universities received $8 million. Agresto asked for 130,000 desks from USAID, the *Washington Post* reported, and received 8,000.

While money and equipment were not forthcoming to the extent needed, either from the U.S. government or donor countries, the importance of the educational system to the broader aims of the occupation was never denied. In the journal *National Interest,* Dov V. Zakheim, an undersecretary of defense between 2001 and 2004, argued that education had a basic role to play in encouraging democracy: "It [Washington] should sustain schools that offer non-religious curricula, where these curricula are taught alongside or apart from religious studies. It should promote and fund college-level educational institutions that require English for professional and technical proficiency and should generously fund scholarships to these institutions." It was the administration's stated position that education would play a vital role in making Iraq a successful country and in discouraging extremism and anti-Americanism.

The fate of Iraqi universities following the invasion varied greatly depending on the local security situation and the degree of ethnic or sectarian strife. On some campuses, unchecked insurgents demanded that women cover their heads and sit apart from men in classes; elsewhere enrollment and course offerings expanded. As everywhere outside the Green Zone in Baghdad, security was the paramount obstacle to any semblance of normalcy. It was just outside of Baghdad University that the Italian journalist Giuliana Sgrena—who would later be the subject of a minor international incident when U.S. soldiers fired on her car as it approached a checkpoint—was kidnapped. If the police could not protect themselves, Khalid Jouli, the president of Baghdad's Al-Nahrain University, asked *USA Today,* "how can they protect us?"[3]

In Mosul, the general descent into violence in 2004 brought murder to the university. The rise of sectarian militias and insurgent groups also brought extreme religious conservatism. USAID and U.S. military forces in and around the city had invested heavily in the well-respected university—more than in the other universities of northern Iraq—but the campus still became a hazard to faculty and students alike, particularly women and Christians (who are more numerous there than in any other Iraqi city). In July 2005, Sahar al-Haideri and Wa'ad Ibraheem, Iraqi reporters for the Institute for War and Peace Reporting, interviewed a female professor who had to be escorted to work by her brother. "If he can't come with me, then I can't go to work," the professor observed. "My family worries about me all the time that I'm at the university." In June, the dean of the College of Law was murdered on her doorstep in south Mosul; her husband was slain in their bedroom. Dr. Eeman Abdul-Mun'im, head of the Department of Translation, was murdered to discourage translators from working with Americans. Three of the ten professors murdered at the university were women. Female students wore clothes that were more and more concealing, and even some Christians took to wearing Muslim headscarves. The violence seemed to have a distinct religious dimension: bullets were flying not merely in opposition to the occupation or to the new political order but to the essential liberalism at the heart of the notion of a university.

Before 2003, the system's distribution of students, except those of Iraqi Kurdistan, was the responsibility of the Ministry of Education in Baghdad. After the war, students were given some freedom to relocate to their hometowns for safety's sake. But for an Arab student at a university in Baghdad, or a Kurdish scholar at Mosul University, the option to return home to a place as violent as Kirkuk, say, might promise little improvement in safety.

Once dominated by Turkomen, then systematically "Arabized" by Saddam in the 1970s and 1980s, Kirkuk is also regarded by Kurds as the spiritual heart of southern Kurdistan. Even more relevant to the prevailing unrest, Kirkuk and the surrounding areas hold most of Iraq's known untapped petroleum reserves. Though the constitution of Iraq outlined a plan for the administration of the region, aimed at redressing some of the demographic transformation forced by Saddam, Kirkuk remained a sticking point in dialogues about its federalism, which together with the financial interests tied to its oil provoked strong opinions from both Arabs to the south and Turks to the north. The question of whether Kirkuk will join Iraqi Kurdistan is meant to be decided by referendum by the end of 2007.

The fate of Kirkuk University and its relationship to the city is equally problematic. The university was founded in 1988 as a satellite college to the university in Mosul. By 2003, there were four colleges and since then three new ones have been added— in medicine, engineering, and architecture—as well as numerous departments, including one devoted to "the science of the Koran."

Driving from Arbil, past the old citadels of Saddam's troops, in traffic jams that often provide opportunities for mayhem, through checkpoints and behind convoys, one can get to the office of the president of Kirkuk University in just under two hours. When I returned to Arbil in 2006 to visit friends I'd made the year before and to give a couple of lectures at the university, my former student Trefa offered to show me her home city. Kirkuk was off-limits to many reporters owing to its extreme violence, but to Trefa it was home. I had to trust that I would be safe—with the added assurances of her older brother, a pistol, a *kefiya* as my disguise, and, as she said hopefully, "Allah's will." She showed me her secondary school, the city's famous bridges and its rundown citadel, which holds the tomb of Daniel. I was not allowed out of the car except for a meeting at the university.

Dr. Najdat Kadhim Moosa, the Turkomen vice president for academic affairs, who had taught in Tikrit and at Salahaddin, told the story of his institution's undeniable if frustratingly slow progress. He was grateful to American officials for equipping the university with Internet access and computers, and for not having pressed for any particular subjects or points of view in the development of the curriculum.

However rough the streets of Kirkuk may have been, the university was far safer, and its staff had not yet been targeted by the violence seen in Mosul and Baghdad. "Our students are in harmony," said Dr. Najdat. "It is not a new condition for Kirkuk: many ethnicities have been here for a long time. Society here is in harmony." True enough, Kirkuk had a history as one of the most tranquilly diverse parts of the country—a valid reminder of the historic ethnic and religious diversity of many cities in the north as well as Baghdad. But in 2005 and 2006 Kirkuk was a city in harmony only in comparison with the butchery prevailing elsewhere in Iraq. Intermarriage between ethnicities existed, and Kurds, for example, could still live more or less safely in Arab neighborhoods, but insurgent violence and in particular revenge murders across ethnic lines had also become facts of life here. Admittedly, though, the bloodshed had not yet breached the wall of the university. "Such things might happen," Dr. Najdat admitted, but they hadn't yet. This administrator cited active mediation of problems between students and teachers and concerted efforts to keep politics off campus as the reasons for the peace thus far.

If violence was not yet a problem, development was. Though the university had added colleges, it still survived from year to year waiting for resources from Baghdad and Arbil. Construction of a new campus had been stopped midway because of lack of funds on hand and uncertainty regarding the coming year's budget. "We have to depend on ourselves," Dr. Najdat lamented, suggesting that USAID and American officials were no longer interested in the university. In fact, the Iraqi administration was now looking to partnerships with private universities in the U.S. in their hopes to move ahead. Whatever the regional and federal government might offer them, they were well aware that in the most important disciplines, the teaching of English and other languages, and scientific research, their contacts with American and British universities might help more in terms of human resources, technology, and access to the contemporary academic world. In the hallway from the main entrance to the vice president's office I saw three posters: one to encourage voting and two to promote scholarship study in the United States.

Founded in 1992, the University of Dohuk, in Iraqi Kurdistan's mountainous northernmost part, was the largest education institution to be opened during autonomy. A former army barracks was converted into the College of Medicine, a prison and execution chambers into the College of Education and College of Law. The university's president worked out of an ornate paneled office formerly belonging to the ranking Baathist official in Dohuk. By the end of the decade, however, this progress was undercut by a rise of religious extremism on campus. A College of Sharia connected to the university had succeeded in gaining funding from an outside group, an organization in Saudi Arabia.

Dr. Asmat Khalid, the president of the university, who had been there since the university's inception, told me, "They were on their way. Indirectly, yes, always struggling against the government. It was a danger in the future." In 2002, he shut down the College of Sharia, sending the students to Arbil and Suleymania. He continued: "All terrorists were one day good people but through education they became extremists and terrorists. To stop this opportunity from any of our young is what I did."

It was not from the study of Islamic law per se that Dr. Asmat wanted to free his students. The canon is open enough to interpretation that the question came down to whose understanding of sharia would prevail and to what degree that understanding would become more than academic.

Dr. Asmat spoke highly of John Agresto and a plan they had devised to establish a department of comparative religion, which would house Islamic studies, along with a conflict resolution center and an English writing center. The plan was perhaps overly ambitious considering the scarcity of resources. Nonetheless, as Dr. Asmat pointed out, it was a way of giving structural authority to the secular voices, which needed to be encouraged in Iraq to counter the influences of Iran and Saudi Arabia. In the most scaled-down version of the plan, he had hoped at least to create an "American corner" in the College of Law. The university received a photocopy machine, a generator, and computers from USAID. Dr. Asmat was not ungrateful but he feared the results of efforts undertaken haphazardly or by halves. "America has paid a lot for Iraqi people and their security, but will lose investment of what they have done," he added, not hiding his disappointment or anger. "We were expecting after the fall and with history of friendship to get some promotions. It is not good to ignore your friends and encourage your enemies."

Contrary to the stereotype of the ivory tower, universities can have a huge influence on the cities and societies around them. This is true in an obvious way in America's university towns, and the effect can be equally dramatic in Iraq, where in the absence of other functional institutions the university can be even more important. The trouble is that where the university figures prominently in the place, the place figures prominently in the university. If violence was not rampant at Salahaddin University, there was nevertheless the strong local sentiment of separatism and the long memory of oppression working against the American hope of a united Iraq.

The new political order in Iraq aimed to redress past injustices in the proportional influence of the various ethnic groups, but the new authorities had taken no steps in Kurdistan to create a forum for a public discussion of the past and the future. In Arbil, there were no school or university programs studying the idea of the "new" Iraq, nor were there new textbooks in the classrooms of Salahaddin acknowledging Kurdish-Arab tensions or suggesting the value of cooperation. One cannot change minds by force; no edict of a mighty occupier could make Kurds believe that in the new Iraq relations with former Arab oppressors would be different. It would, however, have been entirely consonant with American interests and values to do a better job of reasoning and persuasion, to promote a belief in the idea that change is possible, and that the sins of the past can be overcome in a spirit of shared interests and mutual respect. For all the American resources poured into the Iraq project, the relative lack of formal reconciliation efforts came to seem a most saddening miscalculation.

The suicide bombers who have struck in Europe, like the perpetrators of September 11, are proof that a secular university education is no panacea for extremism. The university cannot by any means claim a monopoly in the economy of ideas, whether in the West or the Middle East. But ideas are not without social and economic underpinnings. If the conditions engendering extremism can reasonably be resisted in Iraq, it will depend on the sort of expansion of opportunity and human productive capacity that only the more general availability of a relevant and rigorous education can create.

At the beginning of 2006, almost immediately following the December elections, when I quietly returned to Arbil to give some lectures at the university, a young woman in an English class asked what I thought of America's presence in Iraq. Before I could answer, a young man in a neon orange top asked me if I knew his friend Justin in America. Before I could answer, he said matter-of-factly, "America can go home from Iraq. But we have no control over our fate, our future."

"How many of you," I asked, "voted in the recent elections?" Every hand save one went up.

"How many of you feel you will have the jobs you want or opportunities in the future?" Only one hand went up. The lone student with her hand raised answered, "We all have to be teachers. For me it's okay, but others want to do other things." As things stood, there weren't the resources to learn how to do those other things, let alone find or create the situations in which to do them.

The young *mamosta* of the class interrupted. "You know what we have here for Iraq and Kurdistan as a synonym?" he asked. "Futureless," he said.

I had heard it put more euphemistically before. A year had passed, and this time the message was blunter.

11. English III: Finals—The Beginning of the End or the End of the Beginning?

Life has two days: one peace, one wariness. And has two
sides: worry and happiness.

—*"The Story of the Merchant and the Demon,"*
The Arabian Nights

"THERE is a general theory that music in the East is a crying
woman and in the West the tones of an excited man. What we
can learn from the West is to mix, mix as we want to. We will
sing about hope and that is one way we will change minds." So
Mahir the pop star began his final presentation. He continued,
"Nobody who listens to music or likes the music will blow themselves up. We can improve the minds and help make them like
the world."

Right at the outset, the normally reserved Dr. Abdullah interrupted to point out an exception. "Excuse me, but Western
music has Oprah too." As the class enjoyed a general laugh at Dr.
Abdullah's confusion of a centuries-old European musical form
with an American entrepreneur and talk-show host, Mahir
waited patiently to start again. Born in Rowanduz, a picturesque
Kurdish town some three hours from Arbil in the direction of
Iran, Mahir was the son of a strict imam who considered music
evil. Generational conflict over values, a son ignoring his university studies to start a band, only to achieve improbable success
and with it, to a certain degree, vindication: Mahir's biography
was the story of many musicians and artists around the world
who've made it. An attraction to music had moved him to reject
his obligations of filial obedience and piety. But he approached

singing not only as an art or a profession, but as a way to address society's problems.

"In Western music you can make harmony between two halftones or whole tones, but in our scales we have many divisions and we can't make harmony between them. It's like with red and yellow you make harmony." He continued, fully aware of the implied analogy, "but we have yellow and red and blue and they can't mix to make harmony."

For Mahir, cultures, like colors, were not always condemned to clash—the art was in creating the vibrant counterpoint, the pleasing syncopation rather than the violent dissonance. He spoke of "East" and "West" and "new" and "old," but not with traditional apprehension or prejudice. Each was special. Each had something to offer. Each could learn from the other. Mahir could see Kurdistan in twenty years, possibly sharing a northern border with a Turkey that had been admitted to the European Union and a southern border with an Islamic Republic of Iraq. Kurdistan was where things could merge, and where the coming together of East and West could produce great music.

"Now there is a new group here that tries a great revolution if they can do it because until now we can't find the harmony to mix. The new Kurdish songs are trying to find new scales. In Western music they can do jumps. In Kurdish music there are always expectations from the tones. In West, anything can follow a 'Hello' that starts a song. We can't surprise and you can," he said, speaking now directly to me. "Here we are always expecting. In Western music you are not."

Change, nevertheless, was taking place, he wanted his presentation to tell us, not only in Baghdad or in the relationship between Kurdistan and Iraq, but in culture and art. "So you're sad, the idea is when you live here. You cannot be optimistic. That is why new Kurdish singers are trying to mix the new styles. To bring us optimism and excitement as well."

. . .

Spring had come. Arbil had been relatively peaceful. A rocket-propelled grenade attack on the Finance Ministry caused no casualties and what looked to be an assassination blocks from the hotel turned out to be the violent ending to a dispute over a daughter's honor. Random rifle shots could still be heard and checkpoints and Kalashnikovs were omnipresent, but signs of prosperity abounded: construction of a new hotel on the Kirkuk road, flourishing car dealerships along the main drags; in the lobby of the Sheraton, scale models of a coming mall. Goran, the opinionated entrepreneur who had joined class in midterm, had me to his offices to discuss funding a roadside stop that would offer both a motel and a water amusement park for children. "A million dollars is nothing in Arbil now," he told me. Kurdistan ascendant. The war seemed far away. Dietmar and I had taken to sneaking out of the hotel for midday tea some blocks away, something that I would not have dreamed of doing when I first arrived. Sarhang, Azad, and I would walk to the falafel stand at the bazaar, where groups gathered to watch the American eat "lower-class" food. There was the sense of a new season, an increased bustle complemented by a relaxation in the surroundings. Perhaps it was just the local version of the sentiment that grips American campuses when leaves first appear on the trees and heartier types hopefully put on the shorts and flip-flops well before the weather is warm. The end of term was drawing near.

Over the final few weeks, each student in my English class was to give a presentation on a subject of his or her choosing. The idea was to allow each to develop a specialized vocabulary and the ability to speak on a topic meaningful or relevant to them. The range of interests was striking. Mahir predictably chose the subject of his musical profession but impressed everyone with comments more befitting a philosopher than a pop star. Sardar spoke less glamorously of vitamins, specifically those pro-

duced and affected by exposure to the sun. Two of the engineer
brothers gave rather dry but accomplished talks on Arbil's water
sources and bridge building in Kurdistan. Dr. Kafea, with nearly
flawless grammar, gave a presentation on the environment which
ended with the topic of noise pollution.

Dr. Khalid, ever the contrarian, quickly piped up: "What is
noise pollution? You cannot pollute the noise and noise is not
pollution."

Dr. Abdullah did not miss a beat. "Yes. You can pollute the
noise. It is what you do in this class."

Despite his dapper suits and other affectations of worldliness,
Goran was surprisingly nervous about his presentation. He'd
met with me outside of class to go over vocabulary, and twice
changed the subject of his talk. Finally he settled on the issue of
media in Iraqi Kurdistan. The KDP and the PUK, the region's
two dominant parties, had once had a reputation of being
accommodating with journalists. At the end of 2005 and in the
beginning of 2006, however, the government and the Barzanis in
particular came under intense criticism when a former professor
of Salahaddin University was sentenced to thirty years in prison
for defaming Massoud Barzani. Though he was eventually par-
doned, the case drew the attention of publications such as the
New York Times and *Time* magazine, as stories of imprisonment
of other journalists emerged. Goran, an ambitious climber with
pedigree and connections and much to lose, ventured to address
this complicated and touchy subject: "Do We Have a Free
Media?"

"Okay. We have free media but not the free media other
democratic countries have and this is one important problem,"
he began. "The media is of some economic or political party
interests. It should shed light on government malpractice, on
corruption taken by politicians—if we are to have a media its job
must be to shed light on this."

"Shed light" was not one of the idioms we had worked on after class, but it could not have been more apt. In dark rooms there are dark corners. Turn on a light and some shadowy corners can remain. Iraqi Kurdistan was moving in the right direction, Goran asserted, working at illuminating itself for the scrutiny of America specifically and the rest of the world in general. It should have nothing to hide. But there were still shadows and screens obscuring some realities. "What do we need to get free media?" he asked, his left hand holding his notes and noticeably trembling as he opened up the subject to discussion.

"We must remove the press from the government. There should be a media for the people," Mahir responded quickly, attempting to support his nervous classmate.

Glancing briefly at him, Goran anxiously continued: "Also, on the other hand, media can be used for personal disputes or narrow political interests. We need to regulate this problem. We need law to protect the journalist from attacking you as well and your privacy. So they can't lie about you. And then another to protect the journalist so he has free speech."

Respect for privacy and responsible reporting: Goran's ideal media would have done any editor of the *New York Times* proud; his understanding of freedom of speech and of the proper role of the fourth estate vis-à-vis government seemed a civics textbook explanation of our First Amendment. The problem in his country, as Goran saw it, was not simply with corruption of such principles but also with a lack of entrepreneurship. At the bazaar, in the shadow of Arbil's great castle, men gathered to read the day's newspapers for free at newsstands. In short, Goran suggested, there was no independent source of income to support the proper independence of media. For an answer to the problem Goran looked not to American examples but to British radio and television: government-supported programming with editorial independence.

"It must begin with government policy to support indepen-

dent news, especially newspapers, and to train our own newspapers and then to educate people to support newspapers
through buying newspapers."

"Yes, you are right," Jihad interjected. "We don't buy newspapers so we can't have ads."

A lecturer in math, who had joined the class for the final
month, added, "Our citizens don't look at our media anyways,
just at the satellite."

"Do you know why? Because our media is not exciting,"
replied Goran. "Government must fear that if they do something
wrong the media will say so. We as Kurds believe in democracy,
and free media is one of the democratic principles, but we don't
have it yet."

One of the most famous images to emerge from the Second
World War was that of a milkman making his morning deliveries
amid English homes reduced to rubble during the Blitz. Don-
ning a helmet, navigating destruction, the milkman was doing his
part to maintain some normalcy amid the violence of war. Nearly
thirty years before, in 1914, a young woman named Vera Brittain
arrived at Oxford University from the north of England to study
for a degree in English. But the Great War intervened. Brittain
did not return for her second year: she became a nurse in
London and at the front in France. The colleges and chapels
of Oxford filled with cadets and soldiers. By the beginning of
1915, her memoir *Testament of Youth* tells us, "war was already
beginning to overshadow scholarship and ambition." Despite the
efforts of Oxford's dons and the allure of its spires, the war raging
across the Channel made study unthinkable.[1] With the thuds of
artillery just beyond earshot, and rationing a day-to-day reality,
Brittain found academic endeavor ill-suited to a world falling
apart.

The students of my English class had forged their careers during the Iran-Iraq War, Saddam's *Anfal*, uprisings, internal war, and finally the upheaval that began in 2003. Some, like Dr. Abdullah, had served in the Iraqi army during the war against Iran; others, like the dean from the College of Education, had served in the mountains with the peshmerga. Most had not been in uniform or seen combat. Their lives were like the milkman's and the young Vera Brittain's; they were challenged by rubble and smoke and death to maintain the discipline and ambition to go on. My students faced, in addition, the ever-looming specter of Saddam. Our every conversation, whether about movies or music, or travel, and even the jokes they told seemed tinged with an awareness of being somehow under the dictator's gaze, and running the risk of incurring his wrath. By his mere existence, almost as much as by the inhuman cruelty that he had actually inflicted, Saddam damaged Kurdish lives, even during the years of autonomy. To live was to resist with countless minor acts of rebellion and bravery. Thus the passion of the mechanical engineer speaking of bridges or of his brother talking about clean water was not merely an expression of energetic professionalism but of a difficult but necessary optimism on behalf of civil society. Dr. Kafea had become an environmentalist in the years when the state's leader was a monster who wished death upon her people and when even some neighbors were to be feared. One had to remember when listening to even the most pedestrian of the presentations that there was nothing ordinary about the circumstances in which the interests and competencies inspiring them had been formed and maintained; such curiosity and independence of mind had survived three very difficult decades.

Culture, too, had been an obstacle. Jihad spoke of the efforts of his land-mine awareness organization to educate remote villagers, and specifically how they had adapted their approaches to the local mores. He used a PowerPoint presentation to illustrate how his employees built trust and respect, enabling his organization to reach even the cloistered young women in the villages through special sessions conducted by female employees.

Though the women in the English class had often been hesitant to speak of politics, Seyran gave a talk on Kurdish history, an eloquent and well-researched account of Kurdish efforts at nation building. Dr. Khalid interrupted her, as did Dr. Bokhari of the political science department. The normally reserved dean of the College of Education commented as well. "But, what happened in 1937?" "You should tell us about what Kissinger did with Iran and the Kurds." "There should be more said about Turkey." Perhaps these older men did not think she should have been treading in this realm. But Seyran persisted, and her husband, Mahir, though clearly nervous, stood up for her, as did Dr. Kafea, Bahadin, and I. She had dared speak outside her area of expertise, but she was interested in her subject, well informed, and engaging. She had every right to her views, and would not be made to feel otherwise.

"In the name of Allah," Trefa began her report, looking out on a class composed almost entirely of men. "I want to talk about a horrible disease called AIDS. Acquired Immunodeficiency Syndrome. My presentation is HIV and AIDS and how we stop them. I want to start with this statement: 'The Prevention is better than the Treatment.'" She wrote the statement on the board.

The older Mohammed had given a presentation on the Koranic foundations for Islamic law. His effort illustrated the degree to which the most basic and profound religious ideas could be discussed among the devout and the disillusioned alike. It was a presentation lit twice over, by the unwavering light of Mohammed's faith, but also by his intelligence and knowledge, and his willingness to apply systematic and reasoned thought to a complicated subject. It showed how the Koran could show the way in life without recourse to oppressive ideologies.

Trefa's report concerned how to avoid letting a view of the law prevent our doing what justice and goodness demand. "This is a disastrous disease called AIDS. The first case that we know of was a French airplane attendant in Los Angeles. HIV, which causes AIDS, is spread in three ways. Okay, how is it spread?" she asked authoritatively, with none of the fidgeting or nervousness that had accompanied Goran's or Jihad's reports. She was admirably unflinching in the face of the aspects of the disease that were least easily discussed in her society.

"It started with homosexual sex," she began again, "you know what that is? Contact with infected blood like using drugs with the same needle or at blood transfusion. Mother to child. The rate of infection depends on age and sex, and women are . . . usually can get it from males as there is higher concentration in semen."

Trefa thought of herself as a scientist. She had excelled in biology as an undergraduate and taught a range of science courses at the university. She was also devoutly religious. In her view, AIDS had a scientific explanation and required social action, and even though religion rightly dictated most aspects of individual conduct, there was no need for religion and science to come into conflict. She continued: "Prevention is most effective way to stop the disease. It's best treatment. For this there are many education programs also—like safe-sex intercourse, keeping just one partner, or the proper way to use a condom, how to put on the sheath that can be used to stop the disease."

She concluded, "There is a social stigma—it is a secret disease." So stigmatized, apparently, that nobody else in class would engage her in the subject. I asked a couple of questions, but got the impression that the disease was either too great a taboo or deemed irrelevant. Just before we concluded the class, Jihad offered up one thought on AIDS in Iraq.

"Sure it is here," he said. "The borders are open. The terrorists bring it in."

War, dictatorship, and terrorism have reached into every part of Iraq, and the residents of Arbil have suffered from them all. They were targets of Saddam's helicopters and his shells, of his propaganda and his secret police. They are still targets of Al Qaeda in Iraq and extremist groups within their own cities.

With the invasion of 2003 and the subsequent capture of Saddam Hussein, a great and lingering fear was lifted. Autonomy in the 1990s had brought with it relative safety, but the threat from the south had never entirely faded. "Our life starts now" had been the refrain earlier in the term. But plenty of living had been defiantly done before this start of life. Mahir and Seyran had fallen in love and started a family. Bahadin returned to visit his aging father in Koa, a two-hour drive each way, twice a week. Dr. Khalid had reinvented himself and proved his worth as a teacher. Dr. Kafea, the engineers, and the businessmen had all found and pursued intellectual interests as best they could. Despite violence and limited choices, the will to carry on with a full life was not extinguished in these people who might have seemed more ordinary under more ordinary circumstances.

Upon receiving the 1949 Nobel Prize for Literature, William Faulkner reflected on the effects of fear and violence, specifically the threat of nuclear war, upon the writer:

> Our tragedy today is a general and universal physical fear so long sustained by now that we can even bear it . . . There is only one question: When will I be blown up? . . . He [the writer] must teach himself that the basest of all things is to be

afraid; and, teaching himself that, forget it forever, leaving no
room in his workshop for anything but the old verities and
truths of the heart, the old universal truths lacking which any
story is ephemeral and doomed—love and honor and pity and
pride and compassion and sacrifice.[2]

Love and honor and pity and pride and compassion and sacrifice. These students of English had not achieved the perfect forgetting of fear that Faulkner prescribed. But in making the
stories of their individual lives they had managed to avoid lives
limited only to the basest of things.

On the first Wednesday of April 2005, about a month before
classes were to end, Jalal Talabani was officially named the new
president of Iraq. A decade and a half before, with an eye toward
a cease-fire, Saddam Hussein had offered amnesty to all peshmerga and Kurdish leaders—to all of them, that is, except
Talabani. The price on his head remained.

In Arbil it was a warm day, the wind coming without any of
the sharpness of winter. The sky was unclouded and the dust that
normally swirls at dusk had subsided, leaving the streets to the
revelers. More than two hundred miles south, Saddam Hussein
sat, as he had for over a year now, in his prison cell at a U.S.-run
security facility on the outskirts of Baghdad. There were news
reports of the comforts he still enjoyed in his diminished state.
But both the intimidating figure of so many mass rallies and the
mangy, emaciated fugitive who had climbed out of the spider
hole near Tikrit had disappeared, and Saddam was nowhere to
be seen as he passed his days writing poetry and planning his
defense. Though he was allowed some books, he lived in a news
vacuum, largely unaware of the details of the democratic process
and daily violence that had been taking place in Iraq since his
capture. On this day, however, the human rights minister of Iraq
arranged for U.S. soldiers to place a television in Saddam's cell,
allowing him to watch a video of Talabani's acceptance speech.

The former dictator, according to the minister, was "clearly upset."

The position of president of Iraq is largely symbolic, but Talabani has put it to powerful use. In his constituency of Suleymania and in Arbil, people took to the streets immediately. Fire trucks circled the Kurdish capital with their lights on and sirens blaring, and taxis, rented out for the day, formed convoys that moved through the city honking and waving pictures of Mum Jalal and the legendary Kurdish leader Mustafa Barzani. Flatbed trucks were emptied of their construction material and lines of Kurds, ten, twenty, thirty in a chain, danced on the slow-moving vehicles. Pickups followed like little brothers, young men hanging out of windows and crammed into the beds. A general warning against celebratory gunfire had been issued by the city government and was respected for the most part, but this was a special day. Flags flew everywhere, flapping from the four corners of cars up from Kirkuk and draped down the noses of donkeys trotted in from outlying villages. In much of Iraq, security concerns dictated that U.S. convoys forcibly maintain a buffer zone between their vehicles and other cars. But on this day, the city's residents approached the American Humvees to pass the soldiers Kurdish flags and pictures of Mustafa Barzani.

I did not see a single Iraqi flag.

In Baghdad, Mum Jalal had delivered his acceptance speech in front of a large Iraqi flag. He thanked George Bush and Tony Blair, delivered a stern warning to Syria, and used the phrase "we Iraqis" repeatedly. When officially inaugurated, he would again share the stage with the three green stars and red, black, and white stripes of the Iraqi flag. In Arbil, as in the rest of Iraqi Kurdistan, all was sun, the one at the center of the Kurdish flag, framed by bars of light green, white, and red.

History class was cancelled, as it would be again four days later in honor of the second anniversary of Saddam's fall, and only a handful of students had made it to the Language Center.

Seyran and Mahir arrived on time, as did Azad, the concrete producer, and the soft-spoken Dr. Abdullah. Trefa also negotiated the traffic to make it to class.

As we gathered before entering the classroom, each student individually sought my congratulations. They were all aglow, and class or no, they were not going to let the day's glory go unacknowledged, especially by a foreigner. Today was the end of a beginning, the culmination of the first—and for all anyone then knew, perhaps the last—period of Kurdish involvement in an Iraqi democracy. Over a quick tea, I asked Dr. Abdullah what Talabani would have to do to be a successful president. He looked surprised at the mere thought that such a result might require something of Mum Jalal, but then he answered.

"Last year Ghazi al-Yawer married a Kurd," he began, alluding to the interim president's September 2004 wedding to a prominent and respected Kurdish politician. "Well, Yawer is an Arab and he married a Kurd. Mum Jalal has to take an Arab wife."

I reminded Dr. Abdullah that Talabani already had a very visible and formidable wife, but this seemed of no consequence to Dr. Abdullah. "So you're telling me," I continued, "all Talabani has to do to be a success is to take an Arab for a second wife?"

"Yes. If he takes the second wife like he should, and she is Arab, or even more Arabs for more wives, then he will have done good."

I was as befuddled by Dr. Abdullah's answer as I was by the scene in the street. The city's residents were celebrating the Kurdish assumption of the presidency of a country they did not seem to want to be a part of. So as class began, I put the question to them: "I thought you do not want to be part of Iraq?"

Jihad, who had quietly slipped into class late, suddenly made his presence known by answering excitedly, "Yes, for now we are part. We take slow steps now."

All were in agreement. Dr. Kafea expanded on the thought:

"We have been for a long time under Saddam and under others and now we are no longer under. That is what we celebrate."

"This is a new beginning," added Mahir.

The beginning of the end of sectarian and ethnic conflict in Iraq? Perhaps the beginning of the end of Kurdish uneasiness in their dual identity? Or, and just as likely, the beginning of the end of Iraq?

Mum Jalal's new position signified the end of decades of oppression, and a feather in the people's cap besides, but Kurdish eyes remained set on a different prize that had been longer sought: an independent Kurdistan. That there might be more blood, even a full-blown civil war, was no matter that day. Wherever things were headed, the process had begun. Once the peshmerga had fought in the mountains for independence; now they policed checkpoints dividing Arab Iraq from Iraqi Kurdistan. Once Kurdish leaders had issued proclamations of independence from Iran; now hopes in the north were focused on slowly working toward their own state through the parliaments in Arbil and Baghdad.

Talabani would ex officio have the power of life or death in the event of Saddam's conviction, and from the beginning the death sentence was a strong possibility. Not a single student in my class wanted to see that, however. "Saddam can spend the rest of his life in prison," Seyran noted. "We don't need to hang him." There had been enough bloodshed, and progress did not demand more. Despite the corrosive effects of Saddam's brutality on the individual sensibilities of the Iraqi people—chronic fear and paranoia, the lost work ethic, deference to authority, and an inveterate pessimism—the taste for blood had not taken hold of this small handful of students. The struggle, they hoped, would be less with the past, more with the future.

12. *The* National Enquirer *Writes; and Ali Finally Calls Back*

WITH the exception of the first week of classes, I had been guarded when outside the hotel by two officers from the Kurdistan Regional Government intelligence service in Arbil. They were, I was assured by Kurdish officials, a far better option than private security firms or any arrangement involving Westerners: they knew the city, its people, and the specific threats of northern Iraq. Except for our first two days together, when we traveled in a white jeep with a Korean flag and "WE ARE FRIENDS" emblazoned on the side, they helped me move around the city and the region relatively inconspicuously. Sarhang had a younger sister (who, as reported, was seeking a place at the university) and grandparents, whom we visited when in Dohuk, Iraqi Kurdistan's third city. He also had cousins at a local barbershop, who cut my hair. We visited with Azad's former colleagues at the bazaar and with his wife and children at home. Sarhang and Azad protected me, but they were also my passkeys into alleys, back doors, and living rooms where I would never have otherwise had access. They would become two of my best friends in Arbil.

Azad—known as "the butcher," more for reasons of past employment than for brutality—had been with the intelligence bureau just over a year. He was in his mid-thirties with a heavy mustache and a paunch, a token of his time as a well-fed meat carver in Arbil; others in the service who had been peshmerga were leaner. He tended to eat quickly, shoveling great masses of food into his mouth, which always prompted his colleagues to invoke his nickname with affection. Sarhang was nearly ten years younger than Azad, but had already been in security for five years. Possessed of a seriousness beyond his years, he was ambitious professionally and determined to create for his children a world with more opportunities than he had known. Azad joked daily about visiting me in America; Sarhang would have seriously liked to move his family there.

Coming to know the families of the people who protect you makes it rather difficult sometimes to ask them to do the job. I depended upon Azad and Sarhang; however, there were others I knew who needed them far more. Late in the term, I had arranged to visit with the presidents of the universities in Kirkuk and Mosul. It was obviously a much more hazardous outing than just navigating the bazaar, and both Sarhang and Azad seemed hesitant.

"I'll go with friends from Kirkuk and Mosul," I told them, "they can take me. You guys stay."

"No. No, Mister Ian," Azad said, addressing me with the semiformality that they never presumed to abandon. "We go with you."

"Yes," Sarhang added, not shirking his duty even while pleading for the greater good of our trio, "but let none of us go."

It was their job to protect me. It was my job to teach. The moment, however, that people lost their lives or suffered harm because of my presence, the benefits of cultural exchange would be negated. I could only justify being in Iraq as long as I was able to maintain a reasonably low profile in relatively secure places.

One morning in early April, I received a forwarded copy of an e-mail response from Dr. Mohammed, the president of

Salahaddin University, to an original e-mail from the KRG representative in Washington. People back home in the States, it seems, were very worried about me. Arbil had been quiet, but bombs had been going off with little break in Mosul and Kirkuk, not too far away. The anxious queries, the e-mail showed, had reached the KRG representative in America, who passed them on and up through the Ministry of Humanitarian Aid and Development in Arbil, before they finally found their way to the university president—and then, eventually, to me.

It was, in fact, quite an achievement. I never received any incoming calls from the States, as neither the hotel nor my mobile would accept any but local numbers. No mail came in or out of Arbil. When I needed to deliver letters to Kirkuk and Mosul, I had to ask local Arab friends already headed through the cities to carry them for me. I had not seen a newspaper from Europe or America for the length of my stay. A "friend" of mine, however—one diligent, resourceful, enterprising, and, I had reason to believe, genuinely concerned—had managed to get through, albeit indirectly.

Some two hours later, the representative in Washington e-mailed me directly:

> Dear Mr Ian Klaus,
>   Greetings,
>   Your friend is worried about you. Kindly contact him ASAP. His email is: [xxxxxxx]@nationalenquirer.com.
>   Sincerely,
>   Nijyar

For over three years, I had been dating a brilliant Oxford graduate student who had become an immensely hardworking management consultant, and who was also the daughter of a former United States president and a current U.S. senator. Chelsea

Clinton had been nothing but brave and supportive of my coming to Iraq, just as she had been with her friends who served
there in uniform. The tabloids were regrouping for the latest
spate of stories on her. Our relations had always made good
copy: they had already pronounced us "married" and split us up
several times, along with charging us with having an alien baby.
But now Chelsea's father had undergone surgery for the second
time since leaving office and I was in Iraq—circumstances ripe
with possibility for the inventor of headlines.

Involving the government of a foreign state, passing oneself
off as a concerned friend—these actions went beyond the usual
intrusiveness. Attempting to get the contact information for the
reporter, I asked the KRG representative if he could be so kind
as to pass along my "friend's" worried message to me. Again, he
responded quickly and politely:

> Dear Ian:
>
> Greetings,
>
> I am afraid I can only do that with his permission.
> Once I have it, I will be glad to provide you.
>
> By the way, where are you now?
>
> Sincerely,
>
> Nijyar

I never would find out exactly who the reporter claimed to be
or any details of our supposed relationship; diplomatic protocol,
perhaps even decency, required that the official preserve the
sender's privacy. The reporter, to his credit and despite his mis-
representation, refrained from running the story—only to have
it picked up by another tabloid.

When I arrived in Iraq just before the January 30 elections,
Peter Galbraith had informed Nechirvan Barzani, soon to be
prime minister of Kurdistan, and Jalal Talabani, soon to be presi-

dent of Iraq, of my relationship to the Clintons. Did they figure in my being allowed to stay? Probably, but I couldn't say for sure because no other private citizen was asking for such permission at the time. In any event, Galbraith felt a responsibility to his Kurdish friends. The Kurds pride themselves on the relative safety of Iraqi Kurdistan and on their ability to police their homeland. He would have been betraying their trust had he failed to advise that there was the potential for press coverage, particularly if anything happened to me.[1]

Other than Barzani, Talabani, and a few assistants, nobody ever mentioned the Clintons to me except to ask generally about American politics and perhaps the presidential race in 2008. My Kurdish hosts and Galbraith had done me a great favor in allowing me anonymity in country; after all, being an American was conspicuous—and dangerous—enough.

One month into my stay, I had begun writing a column on the American effort in Iraq and on the progress of Iraqi Kurdistan for a small English-language weekly, the *Hawler Globe*. The paper was published in Arbil, and in theory was meant to circulate also in Suleymania, Baghdad, and Mosul. In my first columns I had written about the importance of the Kurds' making a good-faith effort at Iraqi unification and about the responsibility the regional government had now assumed for protecting the rights of minorities. Long an oppressed minority, the Kurds were effectively a local ruling majority. How they treated Assyrian Christians, as well as the Shia and the Yazidis, would greatly influence their image abroad.

In the column, I also thanked the Kurds for their hospitality, for their protection and the help they had provided America in general. I commended their secular approach to government and relatively progressive views of women's rights, two things that the Coalition Provisional Authority hoped to establish in the whole of Iraq. In short, while my columns had a cautionary and rather prescriptive tone regarding the future, they were complimentary about Kurdish society.

The first edition of the new *Hawler Globe* had a run of nearly two thousand copies, a number that increased to around three thousand in the second and third week of publication. In the Sheraton, international journalists took little notice, while waiters in the hotel's restaurant quickly scooped up copies as English study aids. At the university, students who spoke no English politely stopped to remark on my picture alongside the byline and to shake my hand.

At some point, Turkish officials took note. From a Turkish newspaper in Istanbul to one in Anatolia to some unidentified webpage to a reporter in Arbil and an Iraqi news crew in Kirkuk, the story spread that "Chelsea Clinton's boyfriend" was working in Iraq or Kurdistan or Iraqi Kurdistan, depending on the location of the media outlet. "One is not a duchess forty yards from the carriage," Wallace Stevens wrote. One is still, however, a duchess's boyfriend six thousand miles from the duchess. A photo of Chelsea and me at the 2003 premiere of *The Day After Tomorrow* ran on the front page of one paper next to a picture of Muqtada al-Sadr. Other local dailies and weekly magazines ran small items and, more importantly, cover photos. The staff at the *Hawler Globe* respected my privacy enough not to run an article—they even turned down interview requests for me—but there was no putting this genie back in the bottle.[2]

During Mahir's presentation on music, Dr. Abdullah might have confused "Oprah" for "opera," but it was not for lack of opportunity to watch the former. One of the two English entertainment channels received on most satellite dishes in Arbil ran Oprah's show weekly. By coincidence, just days after the papers in Arbil started running the photos, the station re-aired an episode featuring former president Clinton and included a photo of Chelsea and me. Oprah. A president's book tour. A movie premiere. Muqtada al-Sadr. Turkish newspapers. Kirkuki news broadcasts. By such unlikely conjunctures had I, a bit player in the American effort to help the Kurds, been outed in Arbil.

In the *New York Times* in November 2005, Baghdad bureau chief John F. Burns examined with great insight the difficulty of American officials in understanding the machinations of Iraqi society. He described what Iraqis referred to as the culture of "Ali Baba": "Maneuver and guile, secrets and untruths, terror and treachery are, too often, the coin of the realm for deciding who gets wealth and power." Attempting to explain why Iraqi and American officials had been so slow in responding to rumors of mistreatment of prisoners, Burns quoted Major General William G. Webster Jr.: "We get lots and lots of reports, tips and rumors, and we have to sort out which are real and which are not."[3]

Rumors were common currency in my classroom as well. But the difference between the Arbil I knew and the Baghdad of General Webster's comments could to a degree be seen by comparing the output of the two rumor mills. Politics and the always imminent opening of the airport often came up, more common than scuttlebutt about violence or abuse, but nothing captured the students' imaginations like the mostly apocryphal tales of visiting celebrities. I routinely began class by asking what the word on the street was. The responses often suggested that the *National Enquirer* and the *Globe* might do well to expand distribution into northern Iraq. A rumor that Jean-Claude Van Damme was staying at the Sheraton, for instance, lasted for nearly two weeks, growing more fabulous every day. Despite my report of having seen the look-alike in the hotel lobby, my students insisted that Van Damme was in Kurdistan to film his newest movie on the last Iraq war. He was, I was told, traveling with thirty peshmerga and four personal bodyguards, not to mention a massive film crew.

That "Van Damme" proved to be a boom boy with a documentary film crew did not account for the rumor's demise; instead, it was the widely reported surprise visit of Michael Jackson to Suleymania that bumped the action star from the red carpet. Jackson was then standing trial in Southern California on several counts of child molestation—but this did not prove to my students that he was not also traveling around northern Iraq. Famous for his exotic retreats, Jackson, my students hoped, might have been checking out properties in Kurdistan; this would finally put the region on the map. As the season of celebrity continued, Michael Jackson would be followed by reports of personalities as varied as George Bush, Sean Connery, and the Brazilian soccer star Ronaldo.

For all the commotion and chatter, however, none of my friends in this land of exchanged favors ever asked me for an introduction to Van Damme at the hotel. Nor did anybody expect that as an American I could arrange a photo op with President Bush when he was (falsely) rumored to be spending the day in Salahaddin. In such cases personal connections or even contact was not the ambition. Ingenious as it may sound, for most it was enough just to know that the famous faces they saw on television, the world's rulers and entertainers, knew that they were here, that they had bothered to visit Kurdistan.

After the pictures of Muqtada and Chelsea and me appeared and the *Oprah* episode aired, the students in both my history and my English classes began to whisper. Arbil really is a village, and word had got around the bazaar and the tea shops where the papers could be read for free. By whatever means, the luxury of anonymity I had cherished thus far had been taken from me. Only a handful of students ever approached me to ask about the rumors directly; others whispered about the *mamosta*, which in a way was worse because it discouraged the two-way trust that allowed my charges to open up. There were those, however, within the university who saw opportunity. Ali, who would not be put off in conscripting me as an obvious ally, only to drop me when I proved an apparent threat, had again come to the conclusion that I could be useful. On the same day the picture from the premiere of *The Day After Tomorrow* ran in a northern Iraqi paper, Ali finally called back.

"Mister Ian," he said, "where have you been and why have you not been available for lectures?" He was not about to pause and allow the predictable awkward silence on my part. He was forthright and unashamed. "You know, Mister Ian, I have read in the paper, and, well, that is very nice to hear, and, well, I am a big fan." It was not likely that he was speaking about Muqtada al-Sadr. Ali, with his affected accent, well-pressed shirt, and thinly veiled motives was beginning yet another charm offensive on behalf of his essentially good cause. Wouldn't I, he asked insistently, return to the college and deliver another series of lectures on Hemingway? After all, the students had been "asking after me" this entire time. It would not be right, he kindly nudged, to ignore them further. His nerve was, as ever, disarming.

So it was that a week later I was back in the College of Translation with another group of Ali's students and another set of questions about the inscrutable game of baseball. The opportunity to give a second set of lectures on Hemingway to Ali's more advanced class of nearly fluent students, however, was merely the positive manifestation of a very negative development. Upon the publication of the first pictures in the newspapers, Sarhang and Azad came to visit me at the Sheraton. "*Boshnea,* Mister Ian, this is not good." Subsequently published pictures were accompanied by subsequent declarations of displeasure from Sarhang and Azad. The more visible I was, the more connected I was known to be, the more dangerous it would be for me and for them. In conversations with those I trusted most, Dietmar, Sarhang, Azad, and my fellow teachers Djene and Bayan, the wisdom of my leaving sooner rather than later became clear. While all agreed that I should give my students a couple of weeks' notice, none thought I should extend my stay. At a breakfast in late April, Dietmar, who carried a weapon himself and traveled in an armored car occasionally with guards, put it more bluntly: "You should go. It is probably not the best to stay around longer."

Determining the right thing to do often requires one to reconcile competing responsibilities. I had a responsibility to my students and to the Kurdish people who had acted as my hosts. There were, as well, my responsibilities as a public individual and as a private person, the duties of an American abroad alongside those of a son, brother, and boyfriend in a place that had become increasingly dangerous for me. I had a responsibility to Sarhang and Azad. My decision to come to Arbil had brought some of these various responsibilities into conflict; my decision to leave, on the other hand, was consistent with them all. Fortunately, final presentations in English were nearing an end and graduation day was just around the corner for my history students.

13. History III: "Our Flowers Grew Up by Our Youth Blood for Getting Freedom"

IN *the picture she gave me just before I left, Ayam wore the same impenetrably serious look she brought to every lecture and discussion. Even during the class's lighter moments—my attempts to translate Elvis and Kanye West lyrics into Kurdish, for example—she had rarely smiled. Tall, and elegant in her reserve, the only student to wear her hair down, Ayam would soon complete her fourth year at the university and assume a job in a government ministry or as a teacher. Over the term, I had come to believe that she disapproved of my presence. Except when called upon to read, she never spoke in class. She looked at me with what came to seem unmistakably a glare. We do not want what you have to share, I interpreted the look to mean, and your being here is stupid, dangerous, and insulting.*

"To My Dear Teacher," she wrote on the back of her offering. "This picture is our gift, we want to give it to you. We hope your success in your life. From your students to my sincerely teacher. Respectfully, Ayam."

If nations are held to account for their failures, the descent into violence and chaos in most of Iraq after the invasion is a mark against America. Though the fault should be weighed against all of America's activity in the world and against the nation's whole history—which comparisons may be mitigating or damning depending on one's point of view—it was nonetheless a fault I had to a degree internalized. I had taken Ayam's silence to be disapproval. And I had considered her attitude toward me to be somehow synonymous with her attitude toward my country. In both cases my self-consciousness had led me to misread her shy and quiet nature. I had not had time to get to know all fifty students well, and I knew little about Ayam. Muslim-Christian, American-Iraqi-Kurd, Westerner-Easterner, even student-teacher: I had used these dualities, these generalities for describing differences of power, really, to understand my relationship to Ayam. And I had been wrong.

The Kurds are famous for hospitality but also for befriending foreigners; this has always been to a certain degree a tactical necessity. The veteran war correspondent Jonathan Randall describes this tendency well. Befriending Westerners, journalists in particular, has been a savvy way of getting news coverage for an oft-forgotten or overlooked people and their plight. In my experience, in most cases, it was also much more: true friendship was a way for an otherwise isolated society to establish a connection with the outside world. Barely a week after I left Arbil, I received an e-mail from my history class.

> Dear john claus
> we hope that you are doing fine in every things we are every glad to write this letter to you we hope your successin your life mr john claws we hope that you arrived your home land safely
> u.s.A we as the student of kurdstan history depart in artcollege we have respect for you
> actually leaving made our heart to be sad in fact we missed you damy we are talking and describeng you ermently we are talking about those happy times which

we spent with you al ways you are in our heart it in our
memorandum

   at the end we will send our regards with in kurdish
springes flowers because our flowers grew up by7 our
youth blood for getting freedom wehope that you get
our right intntian please tell your country U.S.Athat we
are working very hard to get home land and livesa fely
and we also hope that you will describe kurdish ethnic
in your country

   with our respects
   from/ studentes of kurdish histoty department
   (4th stage)
   salahadden universty
   sardar sahdy

Yes, they wanted me to spread the word of their desire for
freedom and independence, their sense for their country's history of violence, but their "Kurdish springes flowers" were
personal forget-me-nots as well, the spelling of my name not-
withstanding. The transliteration to John or Ivan and of my
last name to Claus or Claws would continue in nearly every
e-mail I received—as would the expression of friendship and
connection to the West and America, which limited English
could not obscure.

   One transliteration of my surname, my favorite, was unique to
Abdullah, who called me Cabose (pronounced like the last car of
a train). Abdullah and Zaid had been constants in my daily life.
Every morning on the way to breakfast through the Sheraton's
lobby and every night returning from teaching, I would see one
or the other. We would talk about the day, about the future of
Iraq, and about the difficulties of being away from home—in
their case from Mosul, in mine from New York. On the day I left,
Abdullah wrote.

Dear caboose

   Really i am happy coz you go back to see your
friends and your family again in USA in the seam time i
feel sad today coz you left us but i know that i win one
of my best friends so i pray to reach your home with
god safe, please tell me when you arrive.

   take care and stay in safe
   hope i will see you again (inshaallah)
   please stay in touch

   all the best (enjoy)   :)

   abdullah

When I returned nearly half a year later, Abdullah was still working in the Sheraton, having taken a position in the hotel's recently opened travel agency. He would, later in the year, succeed in escaping Iraq and illegally entering Sweden—settling far to the north, farther from his friends, his family, and his country's violence. Like Zaid, Abdullah had never envisioned his future in Kurdistan. His country was Iraq; and whereas the history students had written of Kurdish spring flowers, Kurdish blood, and Kurdish freedom, Abdullah spoke of an "us" that was neither historical nor national—it was simply us transplants who made our home in the hotel for a while.

Zaid was younger and more optimistic. He had fled insurgents though he had not been individually targeted by them. Three days after I left, a suicide bomber walked into a police recruiting station neighboring the Sheraton and killed up to ninety people. Numbers can mask the ugliness of these events. Gwynne Roberts, a documentary filmmaker and veteran of both Iraq and Kurdistan, described the scene: "There was a pile of bodies in grotesque shapes, all of them appeared to be young men." Another witness in the hotel was more graphic, describing "tennis-ball-sized lumps of flesh" landing on the Sheraton's lawn. Zaid wrote me the same day. Despite his use of "susette" for sui- cide and other instances of more phonetic substitutions, the hor- ror of the event is brutally clear, and so are his hopes for a peaceful Iraq, especially Mosul.[1]

> hello my dear Ivan how R U ?
>   and UR family? I hope U be fine, we miss to UR
> smile.
>
>   about me I am OK nothing interesting just Susette
> blast near the hotel lead to crashed some window in the
> flour and the victim buddy peaces it found in the hotel
> garden its terrible state happened that day, any way we
> hope to be safe not in Erbil just but every city in Iraq,
> the stutation in mosul may be better than the last week,
> in frankly its time case
>
>   tell me about U in replay and I will be in attach with
> U and dont forget me.
>   UR friend Zaid
>   with best regards

Days before the blast, my guards Sarhang and Azad drove me to the border. En route to the crossing Sarhang received a phone call informing him that one of his friends and colleagues had died diffusing an improvised explosive device outside of Arbil. Other than a brief squinting of his eyes, he showed no visible signs of upset. He described what happened in English and Kurdish, in a tone inured to the violence that was part of his job, though not unmoved by it.

These men who had seen much still could not help caring. Whether they were teaching me to use the Kalashnikov or shar- ing tea with me in their homes as they dandled their baby daughters, it was clear that Sarhang and Azad had wound up protecting me out of more than professional obligation.

Almost immediately after I crossed, I phoned my mother and then my girlfriend. I was not more than thirty minutes into Turkey before Azad and Sarhang called for the first time. "Mister Ian," Azad asked, as formal and solicitous as ever, "are you all right?" That same night, as I explored Diyarbakir, they each called from their homes. Though the frequency soon declined from daily to weekly, the phone calls would never stop. Country code "32" or "96" would appear on my phone, and it would be either Azad or Sarhang asking after my safety.

Two months after I left Iraqi Kurdistan, Sarhang reached me in Manhattan. "*Choni,* Mister Ian."

"*Choni,* boshi Sarhang," I replied.

"Mister Ian, are you okay?"

"Sarhang, I am in New York City. I am safe."

"Yes, yes," he continued, "but are you okay. Is it safe?"

The calls came every couple of weeks. Korek phone cards charged fifty cents a minute for phone calls to the United States. Azad and Sarhang made six hundred dollars a month combined.

If any of my students or friends most epitomized the challenges and hopes of the new Iraq, it was Trefa. Her family made its home in Kirkuk on ground claimed by Kurd, Arab, and Turkomen, on a street where explosions and gunfire were no anomalies. Living amid the violence of the present, she had also suffered from the violence of the past, losing one of her brothers to Saddam's terror—his body never found. Of the handful of women in my English class, she was the youngest of those who would not shake a man's hand and yet the most apprehensive of what the group's conservative Muslims might wish regarding Kurdish secularism. Trefa wanted Islam to play a central role in society and in her life. But she also loved teaching environmental science, and making her own living. On election day in January 2005, she returned to Kirkuk to vote.

Soon after I left, she responded to an e-mail I sent wishing the class well.

> Hi dear Ian
>
> Its too nice to hear from you. Hope you are too fine and doing well.
>
> I be glad to know and hear that you reached home safely.
>
> How is your family, your girl friend hope all are well.
>
> I appreciate that you still remember my Fulbright application form thanks a lot for you did many things for me.
>
> I hope I could see you again because we all really miss you, so when you come back to Kurdistan you will be welcomed again, it's as your home country, then we can not just have a tea together but also we will try to have some FALAFEEL together also.
>
> My best wishes and greetings to your family.

On July 2, 2005, she wrote again.

> Hi Ian
>
> Hope you are too fine.
>
> I want to say to you happy the new 4th of july your country's celebration day.
>
> You know Ian I will start new english course these few days again in Language center.
>
> Best wishes to you and your family with all due respect.

Things in Kirkuk, Trefa wrote in other messages, were getting worse, but she was continuing with her English courses and still hoping to make it to the U.S. or England to study. Five months later, I received yet another e-mail. It was an Internet greeting card wishing me a happy Thanksgiving.

To Trefa, Sarhang, Azad, and the history students, I was not simply an American. I was an individual about whom all of them worried. I was a teacher and a potential advocate, a link to the larger world. Trefa remembered my national holidays. My former bodyguards and Abdullah and Zaid seemed at times to require real-time intelligence about my well-being in the States. Most expressed a hope I would speak well of their country, whether they conceived of it as Kurdistan or as Iraq. Each of them offered a distinctive expression of mutual respect and friendship. And though all friendships do not stand the test of time, on the last day of history class, one group of friends would come to the defense of my personal integrity, my ideas and my time in Iraqi Kurdistan as a whole.

The final week of class was broken up by graduation. Celebrations took place throughout the week on the university's various campuses to another. Parents arrived from around the Kurdistan region and Kirkuk with the graduates' small siblings in tow. One student brought his daughter in a new white dress; another, Peshraw, brought a video camera and a cameraman and interviewed each of his classmates, like a reporter. Guevara wore his best suit and like most of his classmates danced in the traditional line style, arms interlinked, moving among the families.

With so many parties, it was days after graduation before we concluded the last week of our history class. We had got as far as the late 1960s. In the final weeks we had dealt with the various approaches to promoting change in a democracy: cultural separatism, armed action, civil disobedience, and nonviolence. Betty Friedan's *The Feminine Mystique* had a place alongside the music of Bob Dylan. The differing, though ultimately converging, ideas of Malcolm X and Martin Luther King Jr. about expanding freedoms and justice were given equal time. On this, the last day of class, I was not going to guide the discussion. Two short readings, which Bayan the translator would read in Kurdish after the required readings in English, and that would be it.

Bayan and Guevara took turns reading the first passage, each moving twice through part of King's 1964 Nobel Peace Prize acceptance speech.

> Therefore, I must ask why this prize is awarded to a movement which is beleaguered and committed to unrelenting struggle; to a movement which has not won the very peace and brotherhood which is the essence of the Nobel Prize. After contemplation, I conclude that this award which I receive on behalf of that movement is a profound recognition that nonviolence is the answer to the crucial political and moral question of our time—the need for man to overcome oppression and violence without resorting to violence and oppression.

Peshraw, who had interviewed me and just about everyone else at graduation, volunteered for practically the first time to read. The second passage was also from King.

> Sooner or later all the people of the world will have to discover a way to live together in peace, and thereby transform this pending cosmic elegy into a creative psalm of brotherhood. If this is to be achieved, man must evolve for all human conflict a method which rejects revenge, aggression and retaliation. The foundation of such a method is love.

If ever there was a time and place in need of this sentiment— from the creek beds of southern Iraq, where Sunnis floated downstream dead and blindfolded, to the classrooms of central

Iraq, where Sunni gunmen shot teachers in classrooms, to the streets of Kirkuk, where Kurds and Arabs were engaged in a particularly violent period of a decades-long struggle, each to displace the other—this was it. And if forgiveness was not an option, for it cannot always be, choosing not to seek revenge still was.

Twice again we went over the text, and I asked the class for a final time if there were any questions. A young man, who with two or three male friends always sat in the back of the class near the alert and observant Azad, stood up and leaned forward on his desk, hovering over the student in front of him in the crowded classroom. He had an angular face upon which a new beard was growing and he wore a smirk of satisfaction. Without moving a hand, he began a statement in Kurdish that started in a measured tone but quickly picked up speed and volume. As he neared the end of his statement, his friends beside him looked pleased and more students faced toward the back of the class than toward me. Bayan looked shocked. Hawza, Guevara's buddy in front, stood up and yelled something back at the student. Sera looked down at her notebook as if trying to disappear in shame. Several hands went up. Guevara joined Hawza in berating the group in the back. Staring directly at me, the student continued his speech. It was the only time that the class had been out of my control.

Quieting the class, settling Guevara and Hawza, I asked that they let the student finish. Bayan translated as the young man repeated himself: "You come here as an American and tell us about America and say everything America has done is good. You say that the black people and the people from Mexico and Muslims—you say that everything is good for them in America. You are a white man from America and you stand up and say lies about America."

Bayan the student and her friend Sera, indeed everyone in

the class, were staring at me waiting for my response. They did not look confused or ambivalent; rather, Bayan and Sera and their classmates watched to see if I was going to deal with this in what they deemed an appropriate manner—that is, was I going to put this student in his place?

"I'm sorry, honestly embarrassed, that you think that." Hearts and minds—these were the realms in which I had been operating. What I had been trying to do in that cramped classroom was to foster understanding; that was more important than the specific information presented. And so I continued: "If that is what you think, if those are the ideas you have gotten, then my time here has been worse than a waste."

Hawza again turned and yelled at the student. Bayan the translator hollered something as well. Once more, I quieted the group. Given another chance to speak, the student passed, and I addressed the class. "If I have somehow given you the impression that my country's history is all good, if I have simply told a story celebrating freedom and justice rather than brave efforts working toward them, then I owe you all an apology. And to many people at home as well."

At this point, and for the first time, Guevara interrupted me. In turn, leaning in toward the podium and twisting toward the back of the class, he started: "That is not what you have done. You have tried to tell with balance. We know that"—he turned on the student in the rear—"and he is an extremist and he hates America and he is going to hate you. But he does not talk for any of us."

Others echoed the opinion. Bayan whispered in my ear that students simply kept saying that the student in the back was an Islamist and that he was lying. Azad spoke up: "I don't know what he says. You have spoken to us about America and Christianity and Islam and about your country's history and ours. It has been fair and we respect you for that. Do not listen to him. We are embarrassed that he says that."

The young man in the back was not a physical threat. I did not need my bodyguards to protect me from him; on that last day of class my students were the only bodyguards I needed. Teaching in this environment could not be easily characterized in terms of success or failure. All the students who enrolled passed, and all shared the same postgraduation job opportunities. The achievements of private diplomacy and friendship are even more difficult to measure, if they are even meant to be calculated. But the spectacle of students standing in defense of my ideas, of friends standing in defense of my integrity, was all the proof I required that the time, though too short, had been well spent.

The rational mind generalizes from particulars. Our assessments or descriptions of places and people tend to fall into patterns: our sense of a place is based on geography or security; of a country, on form of government and social norms; of a people, on their appearance, their religion, the feelings they express toward us and our actions. Only when we know individual people and places well do we escape this need for generalization.

Our friends, our family, our colleagues are generally the people we get to know well. We learn of their hopes and failings, of their better natures and basic flaws, and before long they cease to be merely members of a group. Individuality even partly discovered is too potent to dissolve back into generality. Of Azad in black, and Guevara the outspoken, of a young woman named Ayam who I always thought was glaring at me, but who organized my farewell party and her smiling friend Bayan—perhaps I should add nothing more than that I was welcomed warmly, listened to attentively, disagreed with passionately but respectfully, protected unfailingly, and sent off as a friend.

ACKNOWLEDGMENTS

A Kurdish proverb holds that it is impossible to clap with one hand. Nothing is accomplished alone. The debts one can accumulate by one's mid-twenties are astonishing—and mine speak to how fortunate I have been.

I would be remiss if I did not thank the teachers who guided me to history, literature, and writing: early on, Carroll Bailey and Tom Hodgson; later, Gerald Izenberg, Henry Berger, and Iver Bernstein. Most recently, Niall Ferguson has proved incredibly supportive of my efforts.

I should also thank Martin Oehmke, Laurie Richardson, Doug Band, and Huma Abedin in New York and Stefan Link, Vanessa Ogle, James Esdaile, and Jed Wartman at Harvard. Professors Roger Owen and Charles Maier put up with me, though they may not have known it, while I was writing this. I should also thank Cyrille Cartier, Sasa Kralji, Azad Aslan, and Jawad Kaderi in Arbil, and Arlington Cottage in Oxford. James Fallows, Leon Wieseltier, David Kuhn, and Bob Barnett offered encouragement. Clark Dougan and Ted Widmer have generously read and commented on various chapters. I owe a special debt of gratitude to Peter Galbraith, without whom I never would have ended up in Iraqi Kurdistan.

Chelsea Clinton and Patricia Klaus never refused a page in need of editing, yet never struck a discouraging tone. To them I owe a great deal, not least for always asking after the project. To my dad and brother, for never asking too much, I am equally indebted. To my three sets of extended parents—those on 18th Street, those on Heath Drive, and those on Old House Lane—I owe a special thank-you for providing me homes while I wrote this and encouragement at just about all other times.

Andrew Wylie was a great advocate for the project, giving me the necessary confidence to pursue it. At Knopf, it is a pleasure to thank Sonny Mehta for the opportunity. Robin Reardon and Sheila O'Shea graciously helped me do the best that I could with it. Whatever faults this book may have are my own; and there would have been countless more without George Andreou. For his extraordinary advice on style, structure, and substance, I am in his debt.

Finally, in a prefatory note to his 1912 work on the Kurds, the great traveler E. B. Soane wrote: "The tone of the narrative may betoken, perhaps, a partiality to the Kurds; and I must admit, that having met from them more genuine kindness—unclaimed—than from any other collection of strangers met elsewhere, I owe them a large debt of gratitude." Whatever tone my narrative may ultimately have taken, I too owe my Kurdish friends an unbelievable debt of gratitude. Nechirvan Barzani and Falah Mustafa Bakir welcomed and hosted me, and Dr. Mohammed Sadik welcomed me to the university. Both have become friends. Djene Bajalan and Bayan Karimi proved the best of ambassadors to a country they loved but were just getting to know. Every smile or laugh I shared with my students was reciprocated twenty- or thirtyfold—to them I owe the greatest thanks.

NOTES

Introduction

1. Joyce Appleby, "Recovering America's Historic Diversity: Beyond Exceptionalism," *The Journal of American History* 79, no. 2 (September 1992), 429.

2. How and Why: Feet on the Ground, Head in the Sky

1. Archibald M. Hamilton, *Road Through Kurdistan: Travels in Northern Iraq* (New York and London: Tauris Parke Paperbacks, 1937), 112, 116, 169.
2. Robert E. Looney, "The Business of Insurgency: The Expansion of Iraq's Shadow Economy," *National Interest* (Fall 2005), 68, 69; James Glanz, "Thanks to Guards, Iraq Oil Pipeline Is Up and Running, On and Off," *New York Times*, September 3, 2005.
3. Ali A. Allaiwi, *The Occupation of Iraq: Winning the War, Losing the Peace* (New Haven and London: Yale University Press, 2007), 254–257.
4. Bernard Lewis, *The Crisis of Islam* (New York: Modern Library, 2003), 8; *The 9/11 Commission Report* (New York and London: W. W. Norton & Co., 2005). The Executive Summary is available online at www.gpoaccess.gov/911/pdf/execsummary.pdf, 16.
5. Mahmood Mamdani, *Good Muslim, Bad Muslim* (New York: Pantheon Books, 2004), 169.
6. T. S. Eliot, "The Idea of a Christian Society," *Christianity and Culture* (New York: Harcourt, 1967), 14, 26–27.
7. *The 9/11 Commission Report*, 48, 51.

3. The First Day of Class: History in the Present

1. For more on British educational policy during the Mandate period see Peter Sluglett, *Britain in Iraq, 1914–1932* (London: Ithaca Press for the Middle East Centre, St. Anthony's College, Oxford, 1976), 273–295; Robert Kaplan, *The Arabists* (New York: Free Press, 2003), 8, 35.
2. Akira Iriye, *Global Community* (University of California Press, 2002), 82–8.
3. Joyce Appleby, "Competing Histories of America," in *Telling the Truth About*

History, ed. Joyce Appleby, Lynn Hunt, and Margaret Jacob (New York and London: W. W. Norton & Co., 1994), 155–156.

4. David Armitage, *The Declaration of Independence: A Global History* (Cambridge and London: H.V.P., 2007), 100.

5. William J. Duiker, *Ho Chi Minh: A Life* (New York: Hyperion, 2000), 323. The speeches of Dr. King are taken from an assortment of websites as I did not have access to any printed copies. Sites consulted include www.americanrhetoric .com, www.npr.org, and www.mlkonline.net, among many others.

6. David Blight, *Race and Reunion* (Cambridge, Mass., and London: Belknap Press of Harvard University Press, 2001), 4.

7. See Blight, specifically pp. 24–28, for more details on the meeting in Savannah and activities in northern black churches.

4. Election Day in a Country Within a Country

1. Anthony Shadid, *Night Draws Near* (New York: Henry Holt, 2005), 17.

2. *The Other Iraq*, produced by the Kurdistan Development Corporation, 2005.

3. Toby Dodge, *Inventing Iraq* (New York: Columbia University Press, 2003), 130–156.

4. Yitzhak Nakkash, "The Nature of Shi'ism in Iraq," in *Ayatollahs, Sufis and Ideologues: State, Religion and Social Movements in Iraq*, ed. Faleh Abdul-Jaber (London: Saqi Books, 2002), 30.

5. Charles Tripp, *A History of Iraq* (Cambridge: Cambridge University Press, 2000), 145.

6. Tripp, 117.

7. Amazia Baram, "The Ruling Political Elite in Ba'thi Iraq, 1968–1986: The Changing Features of a Collective Profile," *International Journal of Middle Eastern Studies* 21 (1989), 459–460.

8. Jonathan C. Randal, *After Such Knowledge, What Forgiveness?* (New York: Farrar, Straus, and Giroux, 1997), 33; McDowall, David, *A Modern History of the Kurds* (London and New York: I.B. Tauris, 2004), 372.

9. McDowall, 386.

10. McDowall, 386, 387.

11. Randal, 39.

12. Kerim Yildiz, *The Kurds in Iraq* (London and Ann Arbor, Mich.: Pluto Press, 2004), 75.

13. Democratic Principles Working Group, the Conference of the Iraqi Opposition, "Final Report on the Transition to Democracy in Iraq" (November 2002), The Iraq Foundation, http://www.iraqfoundation.org/ studies/2002/dec/study.pdf. In PDF format, 17.

14. Ibid., 49.

5. English I: Travel, Globalization, and Hollywood

1. Alexis de Tocqueville, *Democracy in America* (U.S.A.: Library of America, 2004), 33 "bond of language" in "Point of Departure"; 302 "autocratic rule" in "On that which Tempers the Tyranny of the Majority in the United States."
2. Dodge, 160; Mark Etherington, *Revolt on the Tigris* (London: C. Hurst, 2005), 132. Khafaji, with whom I was fortunate enough to meet while in Iraq, subsequently took a job with George Soros's Iraq Revenue Watch.
3. Joseph Nye Jr., *The Paradox of American Power* (New York: Oxford University Press, 2002), 67. Nye wrote: "Attention rather than information becomes the scarce resource, and those who can distinguish valuable signals from white noise gain power. Editors, filters, and cue givers become more in demand, and this is a source of power for those who can tell us where to focus our attention." Fareed Zakaria, *The Future of Freedom* (New York and London: W. W. Norton and Co., 2003), 254. An astute commentator, Zakaria calls particular attention to the role blogs can play in this phenomenon.
4. Etherington, 47.
5. Yigal Schleifer, "The Kurdish New Wave," *The Walrus* 2, no. 5 (June 2005), 15. Rosebiani has made a film on Halabja and as of 2006 was working on one about Kirkuk.
6. Shadid, 124, 29.
7. E. P. Thompson, *The Making of the English Working Class* (New York: Vintage Books, 1966), 13; Boris Pasternak, *Dr. Zhivago* (London: Harvill Press, 1958), 269.

6. The Hemingway Lectures

1. Etherington, 82; Michael Goldfarb, *Ahmad's War, Ahmad's Peace: Surviving Under Saddam, Dying in the New Iraq* (New York: Carroll and Graf, 2005), 65.
2. All quotes from *The Old Man and the Sea* are taken from the photocopied edition: Ernest Hemingway, *The Old Man and the Sea* (Penguin Books, 1974).
3. Ernest Hemingway, *For Whom the Bell Tolls* (New York: Simon & Schuster, 1940), 471; Ernest Hemingway, *A Farewell to Arms* (New York: Simon & Schuster, 1929), 332.

7. Spring Break in the Sheraton: A Country Comes to the Hotel

1. Hamilton, 42.

8. History II: "Sitting in Judgment"—
can a Nation Move Forward?

1. W. E. B. Du Bois, *The Souls of Black Folk* (New York and Toronto: Everyman's Library, 1993), 88, 89.

2. Benedict Anderson, *Imagined Communities* (London, New York: Verso, 1991); Kanan Makiya, *Republic of Fear* (Berkeley: University of California Press, 1989), 83, 84; for imagination and the historian see Georges Duby's *History Continues* (University of Chicago Press, 1994).

3. M. E. Yapp, *The Near East Since the First World War* (London and New York: Longman, 1991), 19–23; Joseph S. Syzliowicz, *Education and Modernization in the Middle East* (Ithaca, NY: Cornell University Press, 1973); Yildiz, 75.

4. Sluglett, 274; Nazih N. Ayubi, *Political Islam: Religion and Politics in the Arab World* (London and New York: Routledge, 1991), 163, 176, 177. A second table by Ayubi includes distribution of sentenced "jihadists." Students are again the plurality at 44.55 percent (164).

5. On the topic of imperial demise or economic limitations see Niall Ferguson, *Collossus,* and Paul Kennedy, *The Rise and Fall of Great Power,* among many others.

6. Walter A. McDougall, *Freedom Just Around the Corner* (New York: HarperCollins, 2004).

7. Langston Hughes, "The Negro Speaks of Rivers," *The Crisis,* June 1921.

8. Zora Neale Hurston, *Their Eyes Were Watching God* (New York: Perennial Classics, 1998), 1.

9. English II: Putting Out Fires—America,
Democracy, Islam, and the Future

1. Jean Hatzfeld, *Machete Season*, trans. Linda Coverdale (New York: Farrar, Straus and Giroux, 2005), 124. It is worth adding another from a Tutsi who had played soccer with the Hutu men who would later hunt for him. He recalled his experience: "I would hear my teammates hunting around my house. It was the same guys who used to pass the ball back and forth with me . . . They would yell, 'Evergiste we sorted through the piles of bodies, we have not yet seen our cockroach face! We are going to sniff you out, we shall work at night if we have to, but we shall get you!' They shouted and quarreled over not catching me. The players were the most dogged in cutting other players" (100).

2. Makiya, 63. The entire "A World of Fear" chapter is remarkable on this subject.

3. Clarke, "No Return," *New York Times*, February 6, 2005.

4. Shadid and Goldfarb both make similar observations regarding oil and particularly the psychological effect of the confounding inability of coalition forces to maintain peace after Saddam's fall.

5. Nobel laureate Douglass North has written on the importance of trust in impersonal relations in modern economies. Institutional systems that breed confidence in impersonal relationships are a key to economic growth, North has argued.

6. Zakaria, 75; Martin Wolf, "Democracy Is the Wave of the Future but Not for Everyone," *Financial Times*, 25 January 2006, 15; Hazem Beblawi, "The Rentier State in the Arab World," in *The Arab State,* ed. Giacomo Luciani (Berkeley and Los Angeles: University of California Press, 1990), 98.

7. Mamdani, 175; Bernard Lewis, "Freedom and Justice in the Modern Middle East," *Foreign Affairs* 84, no. 3 (May/June 2005), 45–48.

8. Clarke, "No Return."

9. Bahadin's reflections on his father's situation bear a striking resemblance to those of the Kurdish filmmaker Hiner Saleem in his memoir *My Father's Rifle* (New York: Farrar, Straus and Giroux, 2005). Though Saleem's father places significant value on education, he ends up an early retiree on a small pension. The narrator of the memoir recalls: "My father had known nothing but war. He was obsessed with problems of safety" (25).

10. While Goran's "dark to light" phrase can be found in 2 Corinthians, 4:6, he never hinted that he was intentionally quoting the Bible.

10. Battles in the Universities

1. The description of the sacking of Baghdad is from Shadid, *Night Draws Near.* The account of the battle in Basra's College of Literature is drawn from John Keegan, *The Iraq War* (New York: Knopf, 2004).

2. UNESCO, "Final Report: Round Table on the Revitalization of Higher Education in Iraq—Conclusions and Proposals for Action," 22–23 February 2005, UNESCO, Paris; Howard LaFranchi, "Iraq Losing Its Best and Brightest," *Christian Science Monitor,* September 2004; Rajiv Chandrasekaran, "An Educator Learns the Hard Way," *Washington Post* Foreign Service, June 21, 2004. Reports vary widely on the number of professors targeted. As Charles Crain reported in "Professors Say Approximately 300 Academics Have Been Assassinated," *USA Today,* January 17, 2005, the Ministry of Education put the number of professors killed at twenty, while the head of the Association of University Lecturers put the number, including administrators, at around three hundred.

3. Sgrena's kidnapping and release occurred during my tenure in Arbil. While most incidents in the rest of Iraq, including Kirkuk and Mosul, barely registered with many in the city, her case was widely discussed. Each person, Iraqi or foreign, seemed to have a different explanation. See author Charles Crain.

11. *English III: Finals—The Beginning of the End or the End of the Beginning?*

1. Vera Brittain, *Testament of Youth* (London: Virago, 1933), 110, 133. See specifically the chapters "Oxford Versus War" and "Learning Versus Life."
2. William Faulkner, *Essay, Speeches & Public Letters* (New York: Random House, 1965), 119–120.

12. *The* National Enquirer *Writes; and Ali Finally Calls Back*

1. The problem of negative press could not be made clearly than after the tabloid coverage in May 2005. The bombing in February 2004, which claimed more than one hundred lives, had received mainstream press coverage, but no more than other bombings in Iraq. Playing on the possibility that I might have been in the vicinity, the *Globe*, a tabloid, ran a cover photo of the bomb site with the headline, "Chelsea Clinton Collapses: Lover Caught in Iraq Bomb Blast." Though wrong, it still was visible in grocery stores around the country.
2. Wallace Stevens, *Collected Poetry and Prose* (New York: Library of America, 1997), 70. The poem, entitled "Theory," from the collection *Harmonium*, begins: "I am what is around me."
3. John F. Burns, *New York Times*, "In the Dark: It's Still a Mystery," November 2005.

13. *History III: "Our Flowers Grew Up by Our Youth Blood for Getting Freedom"*

1. Rory Carroll and Michael Howard, "They Were Lining Up to Join Iraq's Police—but in the Queue Was a Suicide Bomber," *Guardian Unlimited*, May 5, 2005.

A Note About the Author

IAN KLAUS, who now lives in New York City and Cambridge, wrote for publications across the United States while he was in Iraq and Afghanistan. He is currently pursuing a doctorate in history at Harvard.

A Note on the Type

This book was set in Caledonia, a typeface designed by
W. A. Dwiggins (1880–1956). It belongs to the family of
printing types called "modern face" by printers—a term
used to mark the change in style of the type letters that
occurred around 1800. Caledonia borders on the general
design of Scotch Roman, but it is more freely drawn than
that letter.

Composed by Creative Graphics,
Allentown, Pennsylvania
Printed and bound by R. R. Donnelley,
Harrisonburg, Virginia
Designed by Anthea Lingeman